THE MACMILLAN

Handbook of Chess

Chess Books from Macmillan Publishing Co., Inc.

By I. A. Horowitz:

ALL ABOUT CHESS
THE WORLD CHESS CHAMPIONSHIP: A HISTORY

By I. A. Horowitz and Fred Reinfeld:

HOW TO IMPROVE YOUR CHESS
THE MACMILLAN HANDBOOK OF CHESS

By Fred Reinfeld:

GREAT SHORT GAMES OF THE CHESS MASTERS
PRIZE GAMES OF THE CHESS MASTERS
GREAT GAMES BY CHESS PRODIGIES
THE WAY TO BETTER CHESS
CHESS MASTERS ON WINNING CHESS
IMMORTAL GAMES OF CAPABLANCA
THE JOYS OF CHESS
THE SECRET OF TACTICAL CHESS
WINNING CHESS OPENINGS

THE MACMILLAN
Handbook of Chess

by I. A. HOROWITZ
and FRED REINFELD

Macmillan Publishing Co., Inc.

NEW YORK

15   14   13   12   11   10   9

Macmillan Publishing Co., Inc.
866 Third Avenue, New York, N.Y. 10022
Collier Macmillan Canada, Inc.

Library of Congress catalog card number: 56-7307
Printed in the United States of America

The editors acknowledge with thanks the contributions of P. L. Rothenburg to this volume. Mr. Rothenburg, who was formerly the Problem Editor of *Chess Review*, is one of the world's leading authorities on problems and composed endings.

Contents

The Official Laws of Chess[*]

PART ONE. **GENERAL LAWS**

ARTICLE 1. *Introduction*

The game of chess is played between two opponents by moving pieces on a square board called "a chessboard."

ARTICLE 2. *The Chessboard and its arrangement*

1. The chessboard is made up of 64 equal squares in colour alternately light (the "white" squares) and dark (the "black" squares).

2. The chessboard is placed between the players so that the square in the corner to the right of each player is white.

3. The eight rows of squares running from the edge of the chessboard nearest one of the players to that nearest the other player are called "files."

4. The eight rows of squares running from one edge of the chessboard to the other at right angles to the files are called "ranks."

5. The rows of squares of the same colour touching corner to corner are called "diagonals."

---

[*] This translation from the French is the copyright (1953) of the British Chess Federation and must not be reproduced in whole or in part without written permission of the Secretary of the Federation. The Editors acknowledge with thanks the special permission of the Federation, and of Brian Reilly, the Secretary, for inclusion in this volume of the official translation.

1

ARTICLE 3. *The Pieces and their positions*

At the beginning of the game one player has 16 light coloured pieces (the "white" pieces), the other has 16 dark coloured pieces (the "black" pieces).

These pieces are as follows:—

A white KING	indicated usually by the symbol —	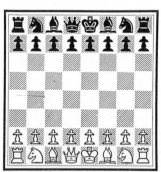
A white QUEEN	" " " " " —	
Two white ROOKS	" " " " " —	
Two white BISHOPS	" " " " " —	
Two white KNIGHTS	" " " " " —	
Eight white PAWNS	" " " " " —	
A black KING	indicated usually by the symbol —	
A black QUEEN	" " " " " —	
Two black ROOKS	" " " " " —	
Two black BISHOPS	" " " " " —	
Two black KNIGHTS	" " " " " —	
Eight black PAWNS	" " " " " —	

The initial position of the pieces on the chessboard is as follows:—

ARTICLE 4. *The Method of Play*

1. The two players must play alternately and make one move at a time. The player who has the white pieces commences the game.

2. A player is said "to have the move" when it is his turn to play.

ARTICLE 5. *The Move in General*

1. With the exception of Castling, a move is the transfer of one piece from one square to another square which is either vacant or occupied by an opponent's piece.

2. No piece, except the Rook when Castling or the Knight (Article 6), can cross a square occupied by another piece.

3. A piece played to a square occupied by an opponent's piece takes it as part of the same move. The captured piece must be immediately removed from the chessboard by the player who has made the capture. See Article 6(b) for taking *"en passant."*

ARTICLE 6. *The Moves of the Individual Pieces*

THE KING. Except when Castling, the King moves to an adjacent square that is not attacked by an opponent's piece. Castling is a move of the King and a Rook, reckoned as a single move (of the King), which must be carried out in the following manner:—The King is transferred from its original square to either one of the nearest squares of the same colour in the same rank; then that Rook towards which the King has been moved is transferred over the King to the square which the King has just crossed.

Castling is permanently impossible (a) if the King has already been moved, or (b) with a Rook that has already been moved.

Castling is prevented for the time being:—(a) if the original square of the King or the square which the King must cross or that which it is to occupy is attacked by an opponent's piece, or (b) if there is any piece between the Rook involved in the move and the King.

THE QUEEN. The Queen moves to any square on the file, rank, or either of the diagonals on which it is placed.

THE ROOK. The Rook moves to any square on the file or rank on which it is placed.

THE BISHOP. The Bishop moves to any square on either of the diagonals on which it is placed.

THE KNIGHT. The Knight's move is made up of two different steps. It takes one step of one single square along the file or rank, and then, still moving away from the square it left, takes one step along the diagonal.

THE PAWN. The Pawn can only move forward.

(a) Except when making a capture it advances from its original square either one or two vacant squares along the file on which it is placed, and on subsequent moves it advances one vacant square along the file. When making a capture it advances one vacant square along either of the diagonals on which it is placed.

(b) A Pawn attacking a square crossed by an opponent's Pawn which has been advanced two squares on the previous move can capture the opponent's Pawn as though the latter had only been moved one square. This capture can only be made on the move immediately following such advance and is known as taking *"en passant."*

(c) On reaching the end of a file a Pawn must be immediately exchanged, as part of the same move, for a Queen, a Rook, a Bishop, or a Knight at the player's choice and without taking into account the other pieces still remaining on the chessboard. This exchanging of a Pawn is called "promotion." The promoted piece must be of the same colour as the Pawn and its action is immediate.

ARTICLE 7. *The Completion of a Move*

A move is completed:

(a) In the case of the transfer of a piece to a vacant square, when the player's hand has quitted the piece; or

(b) In the case of a capture, when the captured piece has been removed from the chessboard and when the player, having placed the piece on its new square, has quitted the piece with his hand; or

(c) In the case of Castling, when the player's hand has quitted the Rook on the square crossed by the King; when the player's hand has quitted the King the move is still not yet completed, but the player no longer has the right to make any other move except Castling; or

(d) In the case of the promotion of a Pawn, when the Pawn has been removed from the chessboard and the player's hand has quitted the new piece after placing it on the promotion square; if the player's hand has quitted the Pawn that has reached the promotion square the move is still not yet completed, but the player no longer has the right to move the Pawn to another square.

ARTICLE 8. *Touched Piece*

Provided that he first warns his opponent, the player whose turn it is to move can adjust one or more pieces on their squares.

Apart from the above case, if the player whose turn it is to move touches one or more pieces, he must make his move by moving or taking the first piece touched which can be moved or taken.

The touching of a piece or pieces entails no obligation if a breach of this rule is not pointed out by the opponent before he touches a piece, or if none of the moves indicated above can be carried out in accordance with the rules.

ARTICLE 9. *Illegal Positions*

1. If during the game it is ascertained that an illegal move has been made, then the position shall be set up again as it was immediately before the making of the illegal move. The game shall then continue in accordance with the rules given in Article 8 as regards the move replacing the illegal move.

If it proves impossible to set up the position again then the game must be annulled and a fresh game played.

2. If, in the course of a game, one or more pieces have been accidentally displaced and are not correctly replaced, the position must be set up as it was immediately before the mistake and the game continued.

If it proves impossible to set up the position again then the game must be annulled and a fresh game played.

3. If, after an adjournment, the position is incorrectly put up, then the position as it was on adjournment must be set up again and the game continued.

4. If during the game it is ascertained that the initial position of the pieces was incorrect, then the game must be annulled and a fresh game played.

5. If, during the game it is ascertained that the position of the chessboard is incorrect, then the position that has been reached must be transferred to a chessboard that has been correctly placed and the game continued.

ARTICLE *10. Check*

1. The King is in check when its square is attacked by an opponent's piece; in this case the latter is said to be "checking the King."

2. The check must be met on the move immediately following. If the check cannot be met then it is called "mate" (see Article 11, 1).

3. A piece that intercepts a check to the King of its own colour can itself give check to the opponent's King.

ARTICLE *11. Won Game*

1. The game is won for the player who has mated the opponent's King.

2. The game is considered won for the player whose opponent declares he resigns.

ARTICLE *12. Drawn Game*

The game is drawn:

1. When the King of the player whose turn it is to move is not in check, and such player cannot make a move. This is called "stalemate."

2. By agreement between the two players;

3. At the request of one of the players when the same position appears three times, and each time the same player has had the move. The position is considered the same if pieces of the same kind and colour occupy the same squares.

This right of claiming the draw belongs to the player:

(a) who is in a position to play a move leading to such repetition of the position, if he declares his intention of making this move; or

(b) who is about to reply to a move by which such repeated position has been produced.

If a player makes a move without having claimed a draw in the manner prescribed in (a) or (b) he then loses this right to claim a draw; this right is however restored to him if the same position appears again with the same player having the move.

4. When the player whose turn it is to move proves that at least fifty moves have been played by each side without a capture of a piece and without a Pawn move having been made.

This number of fifty moves can be increased for certain positions providing that this increase in number and these positions have been clearly laid down before the commencement of the game.

PART TWO. ADDITIONAL RULES FOR COMPETITIONS

ARTICLE 13. *Game Scores*

In the course of the game each player should write down the score of his game in a clear and legible manner on the prescribed score sheet. (See Supplement No. 1.)

ARTICLE 14. *The Use of the Chess Clock*

1. Each player has to make a certain number of moves in a given time, these two factors having been laid down in advance.

2. The time control for each player is effected by means of a clock provided with special apparatus.

3. The clock of the player who has white is set in motion at the time fixed for the commencement of the game. From then on,

each player, having made his move, stops his own clock and starts his opponent's clock.

4. When considering whether the prescribed number of moves has been made in the given time the last move is not considered as made until after the player has stopped his clock.

5. All indications given by a clock or its apparatus are considered as conclusive in the absence of evident defects. The player who claims that there is such a defect should do this as soon as he himself has become aware of it.

6. If the game has to be interrupted for some reason for which neither player is responsible the clock must be stopped until the point concerned has been dealt with. This should be done, for example, in the case of an illegal position necessitating correction, or in that of a defective clock that must be changed, or if the piece which a player has declared he wishes to exchange for one of his Pawns that has reached the end of a file is not immediately to hand.

7. In cases arising out of article 9, clauses 1 and 2, when it proves impossible to determine the time taken by each player up to the moment when the illegality occurred, each player shall be allotted up to this moment a time proportional to that indicated on the clock at the moment when the illegality was ascertained.

For example: After Black's 30th move in a game, it is ascertained that an illegality occurred on the 20th move. Since the clock shows for these 30 moves 1 hour 30 minutes (90 minutes) for White and 1 hour (60 minutes) for Black, the times taken by the two players for the first 20 moves are calculated as follows:

$$\text{WHITE} \quad \frac{90 \times 20}{30} = 60 \text{ minutes}$$

$$\text{BLACK} \quad \frac{60 \times 20}{30} = 40 \text{ minutes}$$

ARTICLE 15. *Adjournment of the Game*

1. If, after the elapse of the time laid down for play, the game

is not finished, the player whose turn it is to move should write down his move in unambiguous notation on his score sheet, put this score sheet as well as that of his opponent's in an envelope, close the envelope and then stop his clock. This move is called the "sealed move." Should the player make his move on the chessboard he must seal the same move on his score sheet.

2. On the envelope should be stated:

(a) the names of the players
(b) the position immediately before the sealed move.
(c) the time taken by each player.
(d) the name of the player who has sealed the move and the number of this move.

3. The envelopes must be put into safe keeping.

ARTICLE *16. The Resumption of the Game*

1. When the game is resumed the position immediately before the sealed move should be set up and the time taken by each of the players when the game was adjourned should be indicated on the clocks.

2. The envelope must not be opened until that player is present whose turn it is to move (i.e. the one who should reply to the sealed move). The clock of this player should be started when the sealed move has been made on the chessboard.

3. If the player whose turn it is to move is absent, then his clock should be started, but the envelope will only be opened when he arrives.

4. If the player who has sealed the move is absent, then the player whose turn it is to move need not make his reply to the sealed move on the chessboard. He has the right to write down his move in reply on his score sheet, put this move in an envelope, stop his clock and start his opponent's clock. The envelope should then be put into safe keeping and opened on the opponent's arrival.

5. If the envelope containing the move sealed on adjournment has disappeared without it being possible to re-establish, with the agreement of the two players, the position and the times used for

the adjourned game, or if for any other reason the said position and the said times cannot be re-established, the game is annulled and a fresh game must be played instead of the adjourned game.

If the envelope enclosing the move sealed according to sub-article 4 has disappeared, then the game must be resumed as from the position at the time of adjournment and with the clock time used at the said time.

6. If, at a resumption of play, either clock has been incorrectly set, and if either player points this out before making his first move, then the error must be corrected. If the error is not so pointed out the game continues without correction.

ARTICLE 17. *Loss of the Game*

A game is lost by a player

1. who has not played the prescribed number of moves in the given time;
2. who arrives at the chessboard more than one hour late;
3. who seals an illegal move or a move so imprecise that it is impossible to establish its true significance;
4. who during the game refuses to comply with the laws of chess.

If both players arrive at the chessboard more than one hour late, or if both refuse to comply with the laws of chess, the game shall be declared lost for both.

ARTICLE 18. *Players' Behaviour*

1. (a) Whilst play is in progress players are forbidden to use written or printed notes or to analyse the game on another chessboard, and are also forbidden to have recourse to the counsel or advice of a third party, whether asked for or not.

(b) No analysis is allowed in the rooms of play either whilst play is in progress or during the adjournment.

(c) It is forbidden to distract or worry the opponent in any way whatsoever.

2. Infractions of the laws as indicated in sub-article 1 can entail penalties reaching as far as the loss of the game.

ARTICLE 19. *The Competition Director*

A person should be designated to direct the competition. The duties of this director are:

(a) to see that the rules of play are strictly observed;

(b) to supervise the competition, to establish that the prescribed time limit has not been exceeded by the players, to fix the order of resumption of adjourned games, to see that the arrangements contained in article 15 are observed, above all to see that the particulars put down on the envelope at the adjournment are correct, to keep the sealed envelope until the time when the game is resumed, etc.

(c) to put into force decisions which he may make on disputes that have arisen in the course of the competition;

(d) to impose penalties on the players for any fault or infraction of the rules.

ARTICLE 20. *The Interpretation of the Laws of the Game*

In case of doubt as to the application or interpretation of these laws the "F.I.D.E." will examine the evidence and make an official decision.

Decisions published in the "F.I.D.E. REVIEW" are binding on all affiliated Federations.

SUPPLEMENT NO. 1

Chess Notation

1. The F.I.D.E. rules recognise at present only the two most generally known notations: the algebraic system and the descriptive system.

2. Each affiliated unit is at liberty to employ whichever of these two notations it prefers.

The Algebraic System

The pieces, with the exception of the Pawns, are represented by their initial letters. The Pawns are not specially indicated.

The eight files (from left to right for white) are represented by the letters from a to h.

The eight ranks are numbered from 1 to 8, counting from white's first rank. (In the initial positions, then the white pieces are on the ranks 1 and 2 and the black pieces on ranks 7 and 8.)

Thus each square is invariably defined by the combination of a letter with a number.

To the initial letter of the piece (except the Pawn) there is added the square of departure and the square of arrival. In the shortened form of notation the square of departure is omitted.

Thus: Bc1—f4 = the Bishop on the square c1 is played to the f4 square. In shortened notation Bf4.

Or: e7—e5 = the Pawn on the square e7 is played to e5. In shortened notation e5.

When two similar pieces can go to the same square, the shortened notation is completed in the following way:— if, for example, two Knights are on g1 and d2, the move Ktg1—f3 would be written in the shortened form Ktg—f3. If the Knights are on g1 and g5, the move Ktg1—f3 would in the shortened form be Kt1—f3.

Abbreviations

O—O   = Castles with the Rook h1 or h8 (King side Castling).

O—O—O = Castles with the Rook a1 or a8 (Queen side Castling).

: or x   = takes.

+   = check.

‡   = mate.

Common Abbreviations

! = well played.

? = bad move.

The Descriptive System

The pieces are represented by their initial letters (but the Knight may be represented by N instead of Kt if preferred).

Distinction is made between the King's Rook, Knight and Bishop and those of the Queen by addition of the letters K and Q.

The eight files (from left to right for White and inversely for Black are represented as follows:—

The Queen's Rook	file	(QR)
"	"	Knight "	(QKt)
"	"	Bishop "	(QB)
"	"	File	(Q)
The King's File		(K)
"	"	Bishop file	(KB)
"	"	Knight "	(KKt)
"	"	Rook "	(KR)

The eight ranks are numbered from 1 to 8, counting from White's first rank in White's case and from Black's first rank in Black's case.

The initial letter of the piece played and the square to which it is played are indicated. e.g. Q—KB 4 = the Queen is played to the fourth square of the King's Bishop file.

When two similar pieces can go to the same square, the squares of departure and arrival are indicated. Thus R (KKt 4)—KKt 2 = that one of the two Rooks which is on the fourth square of the KKt file is moved to the second square of the same file.

Abbreviations

O—O or Castles K = Castles with the KR (K side Castling or Short Castling).

O—O—O or Castles Q = Castles with the QR (Q side Castling or Long Castling).

x = takes

ch or + = check

Common Abbreviations

! = well played.
? = bad move.

SUPPLEMENT NO. 2

Current Expressions

1. PARRY A CHECK.—Placing a piece between the enemy piece which is giving the check and one's own King. A check given by a Knight cannot be so parried.

2. PINNED PIECE.—A piece that parries a check and in consequence loses its liberty of movement is called "pinned."

3. DISCOVERED CHECK.—Check given by a piece the action of which has been unmasked by the moving of another piece.

4. DOUBLE CHECK.—A simultaneous check obtained by the moving of a piece that gives check and, at the same time, discloses the action of another piece that also gives check.

5. SMOTHERED MATE.—Mate given by a Knight to a King the adjoining squares of which are occupied by pieces of its own colour or by enemy pieces that it cannot take.

6. Q SIDE CASTLING.—Castling with the Rook a1 or a8 (Queen's Rook).

7. K SIDE CASTLING.—Castling with the Rook h1 or h8 (King's Rook).

8. WINNING THE EXCHANGE.—Exchanging a Bishop or a Knight for a Rook.

9. LOSING THE EXCHANGE.—Exchanging a Rook for a Bishop or a Knight.

10. J'ADOUBE.—Expression used when a piece is adjusted on its square.

How to Read the Descriptive Chess Notation

The chess notation is a method of recording moves in order to form a permanent score of a game. This is done by combining two elements—the name of the piece that is moving, and the name of the square to which it moves.

To see how the pieces are named, let us have another look at the opening position:

The pieces next to the King are known, respectively, as the King Bishop, King Knight, and King Rook.

The pieces next to the Queen are known, respectively, as the Queen Bishop, Queen Knight, and Queen Rook.

The row of squares on which these pieces stand is known as a *rank.* A rank is a horizontal row of squares. White's pieces are posted on White's *first rank.* His Pawns are posted on his *second rank.* In front of his Pawns is a row of empty squares known as White's *third rank;* then, as we advance further, we have White's fourth rank, fifth rank, and so on up to his eighth rank.

But Black counts the ranks from *his* side of the board. Black's pieces stand on Black's first rank (White's eighth rank). Black's Pawns stand on Black's second rank (White's seventh rank). From then on, Black's ranks are also numbered up to a maximum of eight. (Black's fifth rank is White's fourth rank, etc.)

Each Pawn has a name, too. Thus, the Pawn in front of the King is the King Pawn. The Pawn in front of the Queen Rook is the Queen Rook Pawn.

Each vertical row is called a *file.* The file on which the Queens stand at the beginning of the game is the *Queen file.* In all, there are eight files: the Queen Rook file, the Queen Knight file, the Queen Bishop file, the Queen file, the King file, the King Bishop file, the King Knight file, and the King Rook file.

Each square is therefore named from the combination of the file and rank on which it stands.

Example: In the opening position, White's King Pawn is on White's second rank and on the King file. The Pawn therefore stands on White's King 2 (or K2). The White King stands on White's King 1 (or K1). Similarly, Black's King stands at Black's King 1, and his King Pawn stands at his King 2.

Each player reckons the ranks, as we have seen, *from his own side of the board.* Thus, when White advances his King Pawn two squares he writes "P—K4." (You see here the abbreviations for King and Pawn.) When Black advances *his* King Pawn two squares, he also writes ". . . P—K4."

There is no confusion because each square on the board has two names—its name from the White side and its name from the Black side.

After both sides have advanced their respective Pawns, we get this position:

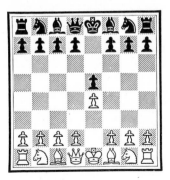

Let us suppose some additional moves are made, as follows:

	WHITE	BLACK
1	P—K4	P—K4
2	N—KB3	N—KB3
3	NxP	. . . .

This means that White's Knight has captured the Black King Pawn.

3	. . . .	P—Q3
4	N—KB3	NxP

So we now have the following position:

Remember that at all times each player describes his move from *his* side of the board. The following diagram shows the double description of each square on the board.

QR1 / QR8	QN1 / QN8	QB1 / QB8	Q1 / Q8	K1 / K8	KB1 / KB8	KN1 / KN8	KR1 / KR8
QR2 / QR7	QN2 / QN7	QB2 / QB7	Q2 / Q7	K2 / K7	KB2 / KB7	KN2 / KN7	KR2 / KR7
QR3 / QR6	QN3 / QN6	QB3 / QB6	Q3 / Q6	K3 / K6	KB3 / KB6	KN3 / KN6	KR3 / KR6
QR4 / QR5	QN4 / QN5	QB4 / QB5	Q4 / Q5	K4 / K5	KB4 / KB5	KN4 / KN5	KR4 / KR5
QR5 / QR4	QN5 / QN4	QB5 / QB4	Q5 / Q4	K5 / K4	KB5 / KB4	KN5 / KN4	KR5 / KR4
QR6 / QR3	QN6 / QN3	QB6 / QB3	Q6 / Q3	K6 / K3	KB6 / KB3	KN6 / KN3	KR6 / KR3
QR7 / QR2	QN7 / QN2	QB7 / QB2	Q7 / Q2	K7 / K2	KB7 / KB2	KN7 / KN2	KR7 / KR2
QR8 / QR1	QN8 / QN1	QB8 / QB1	Q8 / Q1	K8 / K1	KB8 / KB1	KN8 / KN1	KR8 / KR1

ABBREVIATIONS IN CHESS NOTATION

Here are the most essential abbreviations used in the notation system:

King	K
Queen	Q
Rook	R
Bishop	B
Knight	N
Pawn	P
captures	x
to	—
check	ch
discovered check	dis ch
double check	dbl ch
en passant	e.p.
castles, King side *	O—O
castles, Queen side *	O—O—O
good move	!
very good move	!!
outstanding move	!!!

* In the present book these terms are spelled out for the sake of clarity.

bad move   ?

from or at   /

becomes a Queen   /Q

There are times when ambiguity must be avoided in recording a chess move. Take the following situation:

In this position it is White's move, and he captures Black's Queen Bishop Pawn with his advanced Knight. To write this, "NxP" would not do, for the Knight can capture three Pawns. Even writing "NxBP" would not do, because theoretically the Knight can capture Black's King Bishop Pawn or Queen Bishop Pawn.

The right way, then, to record the capture is "NxQBP" or "NxP/B6." (This second version means that White has captured a Black Pawn located at White's Queen Bishop 6 square.)

Another problem of ambiguity appears in the following dia-

gram. If White, who is on the move, makes a Pawn capture, he has to avoid any possibility of misunderstanding.

Suppose White now captures with his Queen Pawn. If he records this as "PxP," we are baffled. How do we know which Pawn captured which?

The right way to record the move would be: "QPxP." This tells us that it was White's Queen Pawn that made the capture.

In the next diagram we have a situation in which White wants to move one of his Knights to King Knight 5.

To write "N—N5" will not do, because it won't tell us which Knight made the move. So, if the Knight from King 4 moves, we write "N/K4—N5." If the other Knight moves, we write "N/B3—N5."

The next position raises a puzzling problem when Black's Rook at King 6 captures a Pawn.

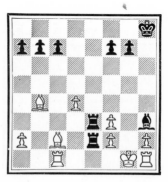

To write ". . . RxP" is not enough, for either Black Rook can capture a Pawn. To write ". . . RxBP" is not enough, either, for either Black Rook can capture a White Bishop Pawn. The right way is ". . . R/K6xP" or ". . . RxP/B6." Then there is no ambiguity.

One last example of how to avoid ambiguity:

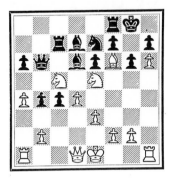

It is Black's move, and he captures the White Knight on his King 4 square with his Bishop. To write ". . . BxN" is not good enough, for the Bishop theoretically can capture either White Knight. So, the right way to write it is ". . . BxN/K4." Then the move is quite clear.

The Values and Characteristics
of the Pieces

The following table, though based on rule of thumb, is the most useful guide we have to the values of the pieces.

KING	—
QUEEN	9
ROOK	5
BISHOP	3
KNIGHT	3
PAWN	1

The value of the King cannot be expressed on any numerical scale. The preservation of this piece determines victory or defeat in chess. In the early part of the game—opening and middle game—the King should be shielded with the greatest care. Be sure to castle at the earliest opportunity, in order to have the King at the side of the board where it is less easy for the pieces to get at him. When enough pieces have been exchanged, the King can at last venture forth reasonably safe from attack. In the endgame stage the King often plays an active role, and he is especially agile in attacking hostile Pawns and defending his own.

The Queen is given an arbitrary value of 9 points.
Thus, a Queen is superior to a Rook (5 points) plus a Bishop

or Knight (3 points). Queen against Rook, minor piece, and Pawn is generally an equal fight.

As a rule the Queen is inferior to two Rooks (10 points). However, in the opening and early part of the game the Queen may be superior to the Rooks, as they are usually developed very slowly. In the ending stage, with the Rooks well in play, their superiority is noticeable.

Three minor pieces (two Bishops and a Knight, or two Knights and a Bishop) are worth a little more than the Queen, despite the fact that the numerical value in both cases adds up to 9 points. This is one case where the numerical scale is a bit deceptive.

Of course, it takes skill to make the three minor pieces work together effectively against the Queen. The same comment applies to handling the two Rooks against the Queen. The reason for this is obvious enough: the Queen has the combined powers of the Rook and Bishop, and the cruising range of this piece is correspondingly huge. Most players rightly fear the powerful darting attacks of the Queen all across the board, and the divergent checks that attack two widely separated pieces. Because of these extensive powers, the middle game is the special domain of the Queen: the presence of this powerful piece creates the greatest amount of tension and complications.

The Queen's attacking power is vividly illustrated in the following diagram, in which White forces mate by 1 P—B6, P—N3; 2 Q—R6, followed by 3 Q—N7 mate.

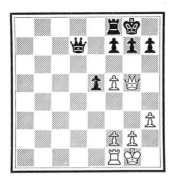

In the next diagram we have an example of the Queen's enormous power of *divergent check*.

In the final diagram we see the devastating effect of a *double attack* by the Queen. Either the Rook or the Knight must be lost.

Another proof of the Queen's power is that it forces checkmate more easily than any other piece (page 57).

The Rook (5 points) is the next strongest piece after the Queen. The Rook needs long, open lines to be at its most effective. Aside from the Queen, it is the only piece that can force checkmate with only the help of its own King.

The Rook is at its best, as has been pointed out, on an open file or on the seventh rank. Most players ignore this important fact by failing to provide for the development of the Rook. At the beginning of the game it is fairly easy to develop the Bishops and

Knights, while the Rooks present a problem. Hemmed in by their own forces, the Rooks will not manage to get into active play unless the player makes a special effort to give them adequate scope. In the games between first-class masters and very weak players, it is a striking fact that the weak players often lose the game before succeeding in developing even one Rook, let alone both.

The best way to get the King Rook into active play is by castling. This kills two birds with one stone, since castling is valuable, above all, in assuring the safety of one's King. Thereafter, what determines the Rook's mobility is any exchange of Pawns, or any capture of a piece by Pawns. When a Pawn captures, it changes its file, and thus opens up a line which can be useful to a Rook.

If the Rook can get to the seventh rank, it is powerfully posted to attack the hostile Pawns which still remain on their original row. One aspect of the Rook which must be watched for alertly is its power of giving checkmate on the last rank to a King hemmed in by his own Pawns. The following diagram illustrates this power:

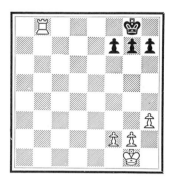

(Of course, the Queen also has this power of delivering mate on the last rank.)

Another important power of the Rook, which it shares with the Queen and Bishop, is the power of *pinning*, explained on page 42.

As already observed, two Rooks are stronger than the Queen. One Rook (5 points) is more valuable than a Bishop or Knight (3 points). This advantage is known as being "the Exchange ahead." A Rook is worth more than a minor piece and a Pawn (4 points). A Rook is about even in value with a minor piece and two Pawns (5 points). Usually it will be the special details of the position that determine whether the Rook is superior, or else the minor piece and Pawns.

Exchange possibilities often arise in a game which involve giving up two minor pieces for a Rook and Pawn. This is unfavorable for the player giving up the two minor pieces, even though the mathematical values (6 points) are the same on each side. However, there are nuances involved that affect the calculation of values. For example:

Early in the game, when one player attacks the hostile King Bishop Pawn by B—QB4 and N—KN5, the defender may guard the Pawn by castling. In that case, if the attacker gives up his two minor pieces for the Rook and Pawn, he is getting distinctly the worst of the bargain. Since the game is still in its early stage, his Rooks are most likely undeveloped, whereas his minor pieces are either developed or quickly will be. In addition, the extra Pawn means little at the beginning of the game.

In the endgame, we may look at the same transaction differently. Suppose the Rook has a lot of mobility (as it very likely does at that stage). Suppose the Pawn is a passed Pawn, almost ready to queen, and well supported by its own forces. In that case we would favor the Rook and Pawn as having the better of the bargain.

One final point in appraising the value of the Rook: it is the only piece, aside from the Queen, that can force checkmate with only the help of the King.

The Bishop is unable to force checkmate, and this immediately stamps the Bishop as being less powerful than the Queen. In addition, mere counting shows us that the Bishop has less scope than the Rook.

We give the Bishop an arbitrary value of 3 points, whereas the value of the Rook is 5. This sums up rather well the difference in value between the two pieces.

The Bishop, like the Rook, needs open lines. The Bishop, however, is much more sensitive to the nature of the Pawn position. Pawns may be placed in such a way as to give the Bishop a lot of mobility. On the other hand, the Bishop can be crippled by an unfavorable Pawn formation.

In the above diagram, for example, White's Queen Bishop has a long clear diagonal unhampered by Pawns.

On the other hand, Black's Queen Bishop has no scope at all. Why? Because its potential diagonals are blocked by its own Pawns. This is particularly true of its King Pawn.

This consideration becomes important when we have to determine whether it is better to have a Bishop against a Knight or a

Knight against a Bishop. The table of relative values gives them each 3 points, so we can conclude that they are *generally* equal in value, and you can readily exchange a Bishop for a Knight, or the reverse.

However, as you become a better player, there are fine points that you begin to notice about these two pieces. The Bishop gets around faster, but reaches only squares of one color. The Knight can eventually reach every square on the board, but may take quite a while to do so.

Expert players prefer the Bishop where it is not hampered by Pawns, and they prefer the Knight in positions where the Bishop is hemmed in by its own Pawns. Two Bishops are almost certain to be stronger than two Knights, for the Bishops command all the squares on the board and have a considerable cruising range. (See page 60.) Also, two Bishops can force checkmate, whereas two Knights cannot do so.

One of the Bishop's great powers is pinning. This is particularly noticeable in the middle game, as in the following position:

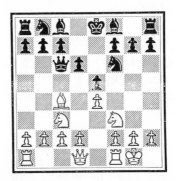

White plays B—N5, winning Black's Queen, which cannot move because it would expose Black's King to attack. This maneuver is very typical, and many opportunities for it arise in the middle game.

The Bishop—and this is also true of the Knight—is generally worth 3 Pawns. Here too there are nuances of valuation. For example, toward the beginning of the game, the extra piece is more valuable than the extra Pawns. A lead in development is of great importance then, whereas the extra Pawns cannot accomplish very much.

In the endgame stage, however, the Pawns may well equal the piece, and if they are passed and far advanced toward their respective queening squares, they may even outweigh the piece.

The Knight, like the Bishop, is valued at 3 points. Unless you are a very good player you need not worry unduly about the relative strength of the Bishop and Knight. However, it is generally recognized now among all classes of players that *two Bishops* are generally stronger than *two Knights;* and that it is preferable to have *two Bishops* rather than *Bishop and Knight.*

As we have seen, the Knight enjoys the asset of being able to reach squares of either color. It also has the power of leaping over friendly and enemy pieces, a characteristic that seems to strike terror to the hearts of inexperienced players.

The Knight's power of forking (page 32) is dreaded even more. While all the pieces are capable of double attack, the hops and darts of the Knight seem to have a mysterious quality which often takes inexperienced players by surprise.

As mentioned on page 35, it is important, when playing out the Knights during the opening stage, to develop them to squares in the center, or near it.

The Pawn (1 point) is, as far as mere arithmetic goes, the weakest of the chessmen. Yet it would be a great mistake to despise the Pawn on that account.

In the first place, the Pawn is the only one of the chess forces that has the power of promotion. Legally it can become a Queen, Rook, Bishop, or Knight. (In practice, when promotion occurs, it becomes the Queen in about 99 per cent of all cases.)

This *potential* promoting power greatly enhances the value of the Pawn, and calls for judicious play with the Pawns. It is also this potential power of the Pawn which makes a material advantage of a Pawn enough to win a game in most instances. This means, then, that a careless loss of a single Pawn may suffice to lose the game; this is the margin of victory, as a matter of fact, in most master games.

Another subtle way in which the Pawn plays an extremely important role is through its unique capturing method (one square ahead to the right or left). Few of us realize that captures by Pawns are the only way in which files are opened. The player who is on the lookout for this will always be able to post his Rooks advantageously on the resulting open lines.

Here is still another fine point of Pawn play. Since it is advantageous to control center squares, Pawns should capture *toward the center.*

Even the low arithmetical value of the Pawn is not quite the disadvantage we think it is. For example, when a Pawn attacks a Queen, Rook, Knight, or Bishop, those pieces must either capture the Pawn—if they can do so safely—or else they must beat an undignified retreat. Thus the "lowly" Pawn can terrorize units of much greater value.

Again, if a piece attacks a Pawn, it can be most economically defended by another Pawn moving into a recapturing position. This suggests a further value of the Pawn: it is the cheapest defensive unit. To use powerful pieces such as the Queen or Rook for purely defensive purposes is undesirable, for these pieces are seen at their best when they attack. This follows from the fact that they have a long cruising range. The Pawn, on the other hand, is static for long stretches of the game. This, plus the fact that its value is small, makes it an excellent defender.

Inexperienced players often fail to realize that the Pawn configuration (or "skeleton") is of the greatest importance. This is particularly true of the Pawn position in front of the castled King. (In the case of King-side castling, this would mean the King Rook Pawn, King Knight Pawn, and King Bishop Pawn.)

As long as these Pawns are unmoved, the King is relatively

safe. But once even a single one of these Pawns is moved, a breach is created in the castled position. One or both of the following conditions can then apply: (a) the advanced Pawn becomes a target for attack; (b) the square or squares previously guarded by the Pawn are now open to infiltration.

The following diagram illustrates the second condition:

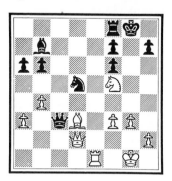

At some earlier point in the game, Black's King Knight Pawn captured at his King Bishop 3 square. This left his King Rook 3 square undefended. (Note that while the King Knight Pawn was at its original square, Black's King Rook 3 square was adequately guarded.)

White's Queen is *en prise.* True, White can play QxQ, but this would be uninspired. White has a really brilliant move at his disposal, thanks to Black's weakening of the castled position. White plays:

1   Q—R6!   . . . .

This threatens 2 Q—N7 mate.

1   . . . .   QxRch

Ordinarily Black's win of a whole Rook would win the game. Not so here, for the mate is still "on."

2   B—B1   Resigns

Black resigns because the only way to stop the mate is 2 . . .

Q—K6ch, allowing 3 NxQ. In that case White would have a Queen (9 points) for a Rook (5 points) with an easy win.

Now for an example of the first condition (advanced Pawn as target):

Black has advanced his King Rook Pawn, which has thereby become a target. This gives White the opportunity for an extraordinary stroke:

1	QxP!	PxQ
2	N—B6ch	. . . .

This Knight fork wins Black's Queen. (Black's King Knight Pawn, in capturing, has relinquished control of Black's King Bishop 3 square.)

2	. . . .	K any
3	NxQ	. . . .

White has won a Pawn.

Like the Knight, the Pawn has formidable forking powers. Here is an effective example of how such a fork becomes possible:

White is the Exchange ahead. He gives back the Exchange in order to set up a Pawn fork:

1	RxB!	RxR
2	P—B6ch	K any
3	PxR	. . . .

Having won a piece by the Pawn fork 2 P—B6ch, White is now a Rook ahead with an easy win.

The following example of the Pawn fork is fascinating because it is combined with a Knight fork.

1   P—K6ch!   . . . .

This obnoxious move attacks King and Queen. Consequently the Pawn must be captured. But how?

If Black plays 1 . . . QxP, then 2 N—N5ch (Knight fork) wins the Queen. And if 1 . . . KxP then 2 N—B5ch (another Knight fork) also wins the Queen.

In brief summary: We have seen that the Pawn has great potential power because of its promotional possibilities; because its capturing method opens up lines for the Rooks; because the Pawn makes the most economical defender; because the Pawn position ("skeleton") often determines the future course of the game; because the Pawn position in front of the castled King has an important bearing on the success or failure of a direct attack; and, finally, because the Pawn's forking power is quite formidable.

Thus we see from all these features of Pawn play that the Pawn plays a much more important role than most players realize. Familiarity with these aspects of Pawn play is one of the hallmarks of a good player.

Maxims for Playing the Opening

1. Start the game by advancing a center Pawn to the fourth rank. If you are an inexperienced player, stick to 1 P—K4 until you feel confident of being able to handle the more complex openings that arise from 1 P—Q4.

2. Unless you can think of a very good reason for moving a piece or Pawn twice in the opening, avoid such duplicating moves. Such repeated moves make you lose time and tend to stop you from developing your forces rapidly.

3. Generally speaking, develop Knights before Bishops. Knights are best played toward the center; this tells you that the King Knight should go to King Bishop 3. As for Bishops, they have a choice of several moves on the same diagonal; allow yourself a little time to make the choice.

4. Despite the great power of the Queen, you want to avoid the early development of this piece. Such early development of the Queen will result only in her being harried by enemy pieces of lesser value. The likely consequence is serious loss of time for you—perhaps even the immobilizing or trapping of your Queen.

5. One of the important goals of rapid development is that getting out your King Knight and King Bishop rapidly will enable you to castle early. By removing your King from the center you will be shielding him against violent attack.

6. Develop your pieces and Pawns so that they control the center squares. "Control" in this context means the power to capture a hostile unit. By controlling squares, you make it impossible for hostile pieces to reach the controlled squares. Since the center is the region of the board where pieces have their greatest mobility, it follows that it is advantageous for you to monopolize as much of the center as you possibly can.

7. Avoid advancing center Pawns beyond the fourth rank during the opening stage. The fourth rank is a good post for the center Pawns. For, once they are advanced this far, they make room for the development of your pieces and hamper the development of your opponent's forces. On the other hand, if you advance these Pawns to the fifth rank, they are likely to lose touch with your pieces. The Pawns become targets for the enemy's attack, and yet they have also become much harder for you to defend.

8. With the Black pieces, you want to strike a healthy compromise between excessively aggressive play and excessively timid play. If you try for too ambitious a goal with Black, you may easily overreach yourself and call forth a White attack that will make mincemeat of your position. On the other hand, if you play too cautiously, you may find yourself in a cramped position that is barren of prospects for you. Hence your play with Black should be solid but forthright.

9. Try to limit your opening repertoire to just a few openings, generally of a simple character. Study those few until you can play them with confidence. Once you have reached that stage, you can branch out into more complicated opening lines.

10. Remember that you need to play P—Q4 or P—Q3 (some time after P—K4) to get your Queen Bishop into play. In openings where both sides have played P—K4, inexperienced players often make the mistake of getting the Queen Bishop out by P—QN3 and B—QN2. This is poor play.

11. In the event that you play B—QB4 in an opening where both sides have played P—K4, watch for opportunities to attack the hostile King Bishop Pawn successfully. Conversely, be vigilant against possible attacks against your own King Bishop Pawn.

12. The move B—QB4 is good when your opponent has moved his King Pawn two squares. This same development is poor where your opponent has moved his King Pawn one square or not at all.

13. Generally speaking, you do well to avoid castling on the Queen side. Once you have castled on that wing, your King is apt to be less secure than after King-side castling. This is especially true if your opponent is more experienced than you are.

14. In making Pawn captures with your own Pawns, capture toward the center when you have a choice. This is part of the recommended policy of controlling the center squares.

15. When you are playing Black, the safe course is to decline gambits, especially if you are not familiar with them. A gambit is an opening in which material (generally a Pawn) is offered for purposes of gaining time for development. Thus, after 1 P—K4, P—K4; 2 P—Q4, PxP White can offer the Danish Gambit: 3 P—QB3, PxP; 4 B—QB4, PxP; 5 BxNP. Now Black is two Pawns ahead, but if he is an inexperienced player he may find it troublesome to contend with White's superior development. Thus the sensible course is to decline the gambit with 3 . . . P—Q4!; 4 KPxP, N—KB3! when Black is actually ahead in development.

Maxims for Playing the
Middle Game

1. Strive for utmost mobility. It is not enough to develop your pieces; you must develop them so that they operate effectively. See to it that your Bishops are not blocked by Pawns; that your Knights are in or near the center; that your Rooks have open lines.

2. Post your forces so that they work together harmoniously. If your pieces are scattered, they can achieve very little in the way of attack or defense. Even if you have only two pieces working together, their concentrated power can be enormous—enough, for example, to create a mating pattern.

3. When you have a powerful attack or much greater freedom of action, avoid exchanges of pieces—unless, of course, such exchanges will lead to decisive gain of material.

4. On the other hand, when you are on the defensive or when your game is very cramped, strive for exchanges—especially exchanges of pieces that are inactive or badly placed.

5. If your opponent has weak Pawns, concentrate your forces on these weaknesses with the long-range view of capturing them, and a short-range objective of keeping your adversary in a passive

defensive position. The two chief kinds of Pawn weaknesses are isolated Pawns and backward Pawns. An isolated Pawn is one which lacks Pawn neighbors of its own color. Such a Pawn can no longer be protected by Pawns; instead, pieces must be used for the purpose. A backward Pawn is one whose Pawn neighbors have advanced, so that (like the isolated Pawn) it is without Pawn protection and must be guarded by pieces.

6. If your opponent has weak squares, direct your pressure on them by occupying them. Weak squares are those which a player cannot command with his Pawns. Consequently you are often able to post a Knight or a Bishop unassailably on these squares. The defender may find, in the words of the great Anderssen, that such a piece is "like a rusty nail in his knee."

7. If you have your pieces well developed in an aggressive pattern, look for threats by which you can menace the opponent's position. The threats may be short term (such as immediate capturing possibilities) or long term (massive King-side attack). The best policy is to combine both types of threats, so that you are working with a maximum objective and a minimum objective. Or, to phrase this differently, try to carry out your long-term threats by means of short-term (direct) threats.

8. Conversely, when you are on the defensive, don't meet threats in a short-sighted way. Try to parry capturing threats, for example, with developing moves or other improvements in your position. Again, avoid meeting an immediate threat with a move that will seriously weaken your position.

9. Remember that attacking possibilities are much easier to fathom if you are familiar with such tactical motifs as the pin, the fork, etc. (See the section on tactical motifs.)

10. Avoid defensive positions if at all possible. However, if you

cannot help yourself, then strive to preserve some freedom of action. If you are reduced to utter passivity, then your chances of escape are only minor. If you can counterattack or offer counterthreats, your chances of survival are much better.

11. Your chances of attack against the King when he is in the center of the board (at his original square) are always promising when the King file is open and when you have a lead in development.

12. When the opposing King is castled, you still have promising chances of attack if at least three of the following conditions apply: (1) you control the center; (2) you have local superiority of force in the vicinity of the hostile King; (3) you have the better development; (4) the hostile Queen is out of play; (5) your opponent has weakened his position by advancing one or more Pawns in front of his King.

13. If you are ahead in development, try to open up the position. If you are behind in development, try to keep the position blockaded.

14. If you are attacking on one wing, it is often good policy to keep the other wing closed so that your opponent cannot counterattack in that sector.

15. If you are defending on one wing, try to counterattack on the other wing in order to divert your opponent from his main objective.

16. In the event that you and your opponent castle on opposite wings, remember that the ensuing play is likely to be of a violent nature as each player advances his Pawns on the wing where his opponent has castled.

17. Doubled Pawns are useful in the middle game, as their presence automatically creates open files.

18. When you are a Pawn ahead, steer for the endgame by exchanging Queens. When you are a Pawn down, avoid the endgame by trying to keep the Queens on the board.

Tactical Motifs

To the uninitiated player it seems that brilliant and forceful attacks more or less "play themselves." The popular view is that a forceful attack is the product of inspiration. Actually most attacks are the product of imagination coupled with routine.

"Routine" seems a strange word to use in this connection. Yet routine, or experience, gives us the setting for an attack; imagination gives us the method. For those who lack experience, classification of attacking methods is an effective substitute. Here is a list of the most common and useful attacking methods:

THE PIN

The pin is an attack on a piece that screens a colleague from attack. The screening piece is the pinned piece. The screened piece is often the King, in which case the pinned piece cannot move. Sometimes the Queen is the screened piece. In that event, a move of the pinned piece is legal, though not advisable; for such a move will lose the Queen.

The favorite pinning piece is the Bishop, and the Rook also does effective work along these lines. The Queen's pinning activities are limited to situations where the prey is immensely valuable.

Kings, Knights, and Pawns are unable to pin.

In the next diagram White's Bishop at King 4 is pinned by Black's Bishop at Queen Knight 2. White's King is the screened

42

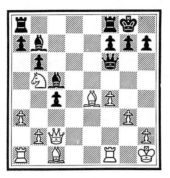

piece.

Black takes beautiful advantage of the pin by playing:

1 . . . .   Q—B4!

White is now unable to play 2 BxB? as his Bishop is pinned on a *second* diagonal. Thus, 2 BxB? loses White's Queen. Such a two-fold pin is unusual—and ominous.

2 N—B3   . . . .

The pinned piece needed more protection.

2 . . . .   KR—K1

This attacks the pinned piece a third time. White's pinned Bishop is still paralyzed and must therefore get more protection.

3 R—K1   RxB!

Removing one of the defenders.

4 NxR   R—K1

Now Black attacks the pinned Knight three times, and White can defend only twice. This means that the pinned piece is lost.

5 P—KN4   . . . .

Despair.

5 . . . .   RxN!

White resigns, for if 6 PxQ, RxR double check and mate.

The pin is the commonest of all the tactical motifs.

THE KNIGHT FORK

The Knight fork—simultaneous attack on two or more pieces by the Knight—is one of the most dreaded of all the tactical motifs. It is also the most common, after the pin.

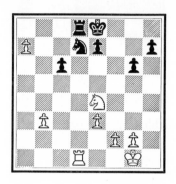

White wants to turn his passed, far-advanced Queen Rook Pawn to account. This is how:

1	RxN!	KxR
2	N—B5ch	. . . .

If 2 . . . K—B2; 3 N—K6ch forking King and Rook and therefore winning. Likewise, if 2 . . . K—Q3; 3 N—N7ch with the same result.

2	. . . .	K—K1
3	N—K6!	R—Q8ch

If 3 . . . R—R1 White has the Knight fork 4 N—B7ch.

4	K—R2	R—QR8
5	P—R8/Q	RxQ
6	N—B7ch	Resigns

The Knight fork wins Black's Rook.

DOUBLE ATTACK

The Knight fork is really a special case of double attack, a form of aggression which is common to all the pieces. For example:

1   NxP!   . . . .

This Knight fork attacks Black's Queen and Bishop. The Knight must be captured.

1   . . . .   PxN

Now White has a double attack with his Queen, attacking a Bishop and giving check at the same time:

2   Q—N5ch   . . . .

The double attack enables White to recover the piece, remaining a Pawn to the good.

DISCOVERED ATTACK

"Discovered" here means "uncovered." When a piece moves and thereby uncovers an attack by a colleague on the same line, we have a discovered attack. For example:

1   N—R4!   . . . .

Threatening to win a Pawn by NxP and also opening the diagonal of his Bishop at King Knight 2.

1   . . . .   BxN?

He guards against the threat but overlooks an even more potent threat.

2   P—Q6!   . . . .

The discovered attack. The Pawn, by advancing, opens up an attack on Black's Bishop at Queen Knight 2. At the same time the White Queen Pawn attacks Black's Queen.

2   . . . .   PxP

Black must save his Queen and is therefore powerless against White's next move.

3   BxB   . . . .

White now wins the Queen Rook as well, and thus comes out the Exchange ahead.

DISCOVERED CHECK

This is a form of discovered attack. When the unmasking piece moves off a line, it "discovers" an attack which is directed against the enemy King—in other words, it gives check.

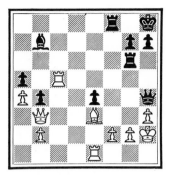

The enchanting feature of Black's combination is that his apparently dead Bishop comes to life:

1	. . . .	RxPch!!
2	KxR	RxPch!
3	BxR	P—K6 dis ch

The discovered check wins. Any move of the White King allows an immediate mate. And if 4 R—Q5, QxBch; 5 K—R1, QxRch; 6 K—N2, Q—B7ch; 7 K—R1, P—K7; etc.

DOUBLE CHECK

This is a discovered check plus an additional check. It is just as formidable as it sounds.

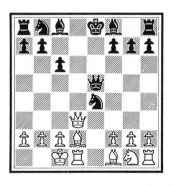

Here is the classic example of a double check:

    1   Q—Q8ch!!   KxQ
    2   B—N5 dbl ch   K—K1

Or 2 . . . K—B2; 3 B—Q8 mate.

    3   R—Q8 mate

THE OVERWORKED PIECE

Just as no man can serve two masters, so a piece that has more than one task may fail in its twofold task. In the following example White's Queen as well as his Knight are overworked:

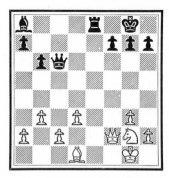

    1   . . . .   R—K8ch!!

White resigns, for if he plays 2 QxR, there follows 2 . . . QxN mate. And on 2 NxR, Black has 2 . . . Q—R8 mate.

REMOVAL OF A GUARD

A piece that guards another unit is a logical target for attack. Undermine the guard, and you undermine the guarded piece as well.

Black's Rook guards his Bishop. White exploits this relationship by playing:

1   K—N3   . . . .

Black is now lost, for if he plays 1 . . . R—Q5 (to keep on guarding the Bishop), there follows 2 N—B5ch, winning the Rook. Of course, if Black retreats 1 . . . R—B3, White simply picks off the Bishop.

Note that 1 K—K3 also wins, for if 1 . . . RxP; 2 N—B5ch is still deadly.

QUEENING COMBINATIONS

Opportunities for combinations involving Pawn promotion are very common. We use the term "queening" because the promotion is usually to a Queen. It does happen on certain rare occasions that a player promotes to a Rook or Knight or Bishop—a case of "underpromotion."

Here is an extraordinary example of the promotion power of the Pawn. White's Queen Pawn is apparently the "candidate":

1	R—B8!!	RxR
2	R—K8ch!	NxR
3	P—Q7	N—Q3

This is the only defense; but an ugly surprise awaits Black.

4	PxR/Q	NxQ
5	PxP!	Resigns

As White threatens 6 PxN/Q as well as P—N8/Q, Black has no defense.

UNDERPROMOTION

Despite his material minus, White can win by promoting his advanced Pawn:

1	R—B8ch!	RxR

Now the conventional promotion to a Queen would leave Black a piece ahead with an eventual win.

2	QxPch!!	KxQ
3	PxR/Nch! and wins	

After 4 NxQ White is two Pawns up, with a won game.

TRAPPED MAN

Sometimes a piece strays so far from home that it can be surrounded and engulfed. One of the most common examples is that of a Bishop enmeshed in a net of Pawns:

Black gains time to trap White's Bishop:

| 1 | . . . . | P—B4 |
| 2 | Q—K3 | P—B5 |

White's Bishop is trapped by the Black Pawns.

X-RAY ATTACK

The X-ray attack, or "skewer," attacks one piece directly, and a second piece indirectly, on the same line. When the directly attacked piece moves out of the way, the second piece on the same line becomes vulnerable.

White gives up his Pawn as he sees a chance to make use of a winning X-ray attack:

1   R—R8!   . . . .

Note that 1 R—KN8 also wins.

1   . . . .   RxP

Black has no choice, as the Pawn threatens to queen.

2   R—R7ch   . . . .

Black resigns, as the X-ray attack wins his Rook.

VULNERABLE FIRST RANK

All chess authorities advise that the King should be castled at the earliest opportunity and snugly protected by the Pawns in front of the castled position. However, this situation contains one potential element of danger. The first rank must be guarded vigilantly against a surprise raid by the hostile Queen or Rook. When the first rank is vulnerable to such an attack, the consequences may be disastrous.

1   Q—B3!   Q—B4

Black cannot play 1 . . . QxQ? because of 2 RxR mate.

Black now hopes for 2 QxR?, RxR with even forces. But White outthinks him.

2   RxRch!   QxR
3   QxR and wins

SURPRISE ATTACKS

Some attacks may occur too rarely to be classified. Their relative rarity gives them an added surprise value which enhances their power.

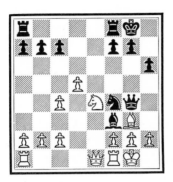

White is reconciled to Black's playing 1 . . . NxNP and regaining his piece with a powerful attack.

But Black has a much stronger move, immediately forcing checkmate:

1 . . . . Q—R6!

White resigns, for if 2 PxQ, NxP mate.

Maxims for Playing the Endgame

1. Know the elementary checkmates, with (a) the Queen; (b) the Rook; (c) the two Bishops; and (d) Bishop and Knight. Such knowledge is absolutely essential to enable you to win systematically, to give you a good insight into the workings of the pieces, and to give you a clear notion of the purposefulness of chess play.

2. Remember that once the major pieces have been exchanged and only a relatively small number of pieces is left on the board, the time has come for your King to become active. With most of the pieces gone, the King is reasonably safe from attack. He can now play a useful role, primarily in escorting his passed Pawns to queen and in heading off the opponent's advancing Pawns or capturing them.

3. Make use of your passed Pawns; they are potential Queens. Lacking any obstructions from the other side, they are a powerful winning asset.

4. In a Rook-and-Pawn ending, strive to post your Rook (or Rooks) on the seventh rank. This is the ideally aggressive locale for these powerful pieces. They menace the opponent's Pawns in the heart of his position, and at the same time tie up his pieces with petty defensive tasks.

5. When you are ahead in material, it is almost always good play to *simplify*—but how? Exchange pieces, because that clarifies the situation, but don't allow too many Pawn exchanges. If you swap down to one Pawn against none, your opponent may be able to give up a Bishop or Knight for the remaining Pawn, leaving a drawn position because of lack of mating material.

6. Contrariwise, if you are behind in material, your best chance will generally lie in creating complications and avoiding exchanges. If you are compelled to exchange, try to exchange Pawns and avoid exchanges of pieces.

7. If you have a Bishop in the endgame, be careful not to place too many Pawns on the same color as those which the Bishop travels on. If the Pawns are posted on this color, two results will follow: the Bishop's mobility will be cut down, and the squares of the other color will become weak because they will not be commanded by your Pawns.

8. Try to centralize your King in the endgame. At a center post this piece is poised for action on either wing.

9. Place your Rooks behind your passed Pawns, so that you can advance the Pawns and still preserve freedom of action for your Rook.

10. Place your Rook also behind opposing passed Pawns as a means of preserving the Rook's freedom of action. If you make the mistake of posting your Rook in front of hostile passed Pawns, then your Rook will be paralyzed by the Pawn's threat to advance.

11. A Bishop is on the whole slightly superior to the Knight, especially when the Pawn position is strewn over the whole board. Here the Bishop's power of rapid and extensive movement

should tell in his favor. On the other hand, if the Bishop is hampered in his movements by his own Pawns, then the Knight may well turn out in that case to be the stronger piece.

12. Two Bishops are almost always superior to Bishop and Knight. By making appropriate Pawn moves, valuable squares can be taken away from the Knight's jurisdiction. On the other hand, the two Bishops have potential sway over every square on the board.

13. Remember that in the endgame of King and Pawn against King, you cannot win with a Rook Pawn if your opponent's King can reach the queening square. Efforts to drive out the King will only lead to stalemate.

14. Bishop and Rook Pawn cannot win against a lone King if (a) the Bishop does not command the queening square, and (b) the opposing King can reach the queening square.

Basic Endgames

The chess student finds it useful to be familiar with certain types of standard endings. These serve as models or prototypes of positions that can often be achieved in practical play. The most fundamental of these endings are the elementary checkmates, with (a) the Queen; (b) the Rook; (c) two Bishops; and (d) Bishop and Knight.

ELEMENTARY CHECKMATES

WHITE TO PLAY

The checkmate with the Queen is the easiest of the lot. White first brings his King near the Black King and then drives him back to one of the sides of the board. Then, when the Black King's mobility has been sufficiently reduced, checkmate becomes possible.

1	K—N2	K—Q4
2	K—B3	K—K3

3 K—Q4   K—B3

Though Black fights back as best he can, he is being forced to the side of the board. Now White's Queen swings into action, taking away still more squares from the Black King.

4 Q—K4   K—B2
5 K—K5   K—N2

Likewise after 5 . . . K—K2 White has a quick mate with 6 Q—N7ch, etc.

6 K—B5   K—B2
7 Q—N7ch   K—N1

Now that the King has been forced to the side of the board, he is mated in short order.

8 K—B6   K—B1

Or 8 . . . K—R1; 9 Q—N7 mate.

9 Q—KB7 mate

White has other ways to force checkmate: 9 Q—B8 mate or 9 Q—N8 mate or 9 Q—R8 mate. The Rook can checkmate only by this latter method, whereas the Queen has two ways, indicated by Q—KB7 mate and 9 Q—N8 mate.

WHITE TO PLAY

To bring about checkmate with the Rook, the White King has to work harder than in the Queen checkmate. This stands to reason, as the Rook is weaker than the Queen.

The method is the same: White's King advances toward the Black King, and then the Rook co-operates to drive the Black King to the side of the board.

1	K—N2	K—Q5
2	K—B2	K—K5
3	R—N5	. . . .

This cuts off half the board from the Black King.

3	. . . .	K—Q5
4	K—N3	K—K5
5	K—B3	K—B5
6	K—Q3	K—N5
7	K—K3	K—N6
8	R—N5ch	. . . .

Always check when the Kings face each other. For now the Black King is driven to the side of the board.

8	. . . .	K—R5
9	K—B4	K—R6
10	K—B3	K—R7

Black tries to escape. If 10 . . . K—R5; 11 R—QR5 (several other moves along the fifth rank will also do), K—R6; 12 R—R5 mate.

11	R—N8	K—R8
12	K—B2	K—R7
13	R—R8 mate	

The mate with two Bishops is still harder. In the next case the lone King must be driven not only to the side of the board, but to a corner square. Close co-operation is called for on the part of the two Bishops and their King.

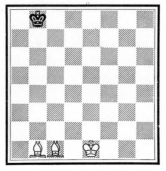

WHITE TO PLAY

1	B—R3	K—B2
2	B—R2	K—B3
3	K—Q2	K—N4
4	K—Q3	K—R5
5	B—B8	K—N4
6	B—N3	K—B3
7	K—Q4	. . . .

Slowly he forces Black's King back. If now 7 . . . K—N4; 8 K—Q5, K—R4; 9 K—B5, K—R3; 10 B—R4, and Black's moves have become very limited.

7	. . . .	K—Q2
8	K—K5	K—K1
9	B—B5	K—Q2
10	B—R4ch	K—Q1
11	K—K6	K—B2

Note how the number of squares available to the Black King has been reduced.

12	B—N5	K—N2
13	K—Q7	K—N1
14	B—R6	K—R1
15	K—B6	K—N1

16	K—N6	K—R1
17	B—N7ch	K—N1
18	B—Q6 mate	

WHITE TO PLAY

Mate with the Bishop and Knight is the most difficult of all. The lone King must be driven to a corner square of the same color as those on which the Bishop travels.

1	N—N3	K—Q3
2	K—N5	. . . .

Precisely because this is the most difficult of the elementary checkmates, the White King has to work harder than in any other type of checkmate.

2	. . . .	K—Q4
3	B—B7ch	K—Q3
4	B—B4	K—K4
5	K—B5	K—K5
6	K—Q6	K—B4

Black fights hard to stave off being driven to the prospective mating square—his Queen Rook 1 square.

7	B—Q3ch	K—B3
8	N—Q2	K—B2
9	N—B3	K—B3
10	K—Q7	K—B2

| 11 | B—B4ch | K—B3 |
| 12 | B—K6 | . . . . |

White has at last succeeded in confining Black's King to the last three ranks.

12	. . . .	K—N2
13	K—K7	K—N3
14	B—N4	K—N2
15	N—K5	K—R3
16	K—B6	K—R2
17	N—B7	K—N1

White has achieved another objective: confining Black's King to his first rank.

White's plan for forcing Black's King to his Queen Rook 1 square is as follows: White's King moves to the Queen side, going along the sixth rank. White's Knight plays N—K5, N—Q7, N—B5, and N—N7 as called for. White's Bishop makes a move every now and then to prevent Black's King from escaping to the King side.

18	B—B5	K—B1
19	B—R7	K—K1
20	N—K5	K—B1

If Black tries to make a break for freedom with 20 . . . K—Q1 there follows 21 K—K6, K—B2; 22 N—Q7, K—N2; 23 B—Q3, K—B3; 24 B—K2, K—B2; 25 B—B3, K—Q1; 26 K—Q6 winning as in the main line.

21	N—Q7ch	K—K1
22	K—K6	K—Q1
23	K—Q6	K—K1
24	B—N6ch	. . . .

Driving Black's King back.

| 24 | . . . . | K—Q1 |
| 25 | N—B5 | K—B1 |

26	B—B7	K—Q1
27	N—N7ch	K—B1
28	K—B6	K—N1
29	K—N6	K—B1
30	B—K6ch	K—N1

The last stage: Black's King is trapped near the corner and White can prepare the mating maneuver.

31	N—B5	K—R1
32	B—Q7	K—N1
33	N—R6ch	K—R1
34	B—B6 mate	

Diagram shows this classic mate position:

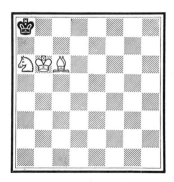

KING AND PAWN ENDINGS

BLACK TO PLAY

White wins, as he has the "Opposition." (This means that the Kings face each other with an odd number of squares between them, and it is Black's turn to move.)

There follows:

1	. . . .	K—K1
2	P—K7	K—B2
3	K—Q7 and wins	

White queens his Pawn next move.

On the other hand, suppose it is White's move in the foregoing diagram. *Then Black has the Opposition,* and White cannot win:

1	P—K7ch	K—K1

Now if 2 K—K6 (to guard the Pawn), Black is stalemated.

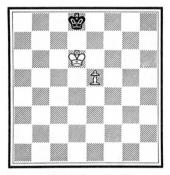

WHITE TO PLAY

Here White's Pawn is on the fifth rank, instead of on the sixth (as in the previous diagram). This means that White can win even if he doesn't have the Opposition. Thus:

1	P—K6	K—K1
2	P—K7	K—B2
3	K—Q7 and wins	

If it is Black's move in the above diagram, White still wins by taking the Opposition:

1	. . . .	K—K1

2   K—K6!   . . . .

Not 2 P—K6??, K—Q1; 3 P—K7ch, K—K1; 4 K—K6 and Black
is stalemated.

2   . . . .   K—Q1
3   K—B7 and wins

For Black is helpless against the advance of the Pawn.

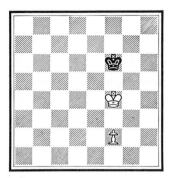

WHITE TO PLAY

In order to keep the Opposition, White must move his Pawn:

1   P—B3!   K—K3
2   K—N5   K—K2
3   K—B5   K—B2
4   P—B4   K—K2
5   K—N6   K—B1
6   P—B5   K—N1
7   P—B6   K—B1
8   P—B7   K—K2
9   K—N7 and wins

White can now queen his Pawn.

If Black moves first in the foregoing diagram, White wins in
similar fashion:

1   . . . .   K—N3

2	K—K5	K—B2
3	K—B5!	K—K2
4	K—N6	K—B1
5	K—B6	K—N1
6	P—B4	K—B1
7	P—B5	K—N1
8	K—K7 and wins	

The queening of the Pawn is assured.

If the White King has not reached the sixth rank and cannot be placed in front of the Pawn, the position is a draw.

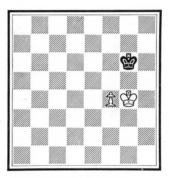

BLACK TO PLAY

Black must give up the Opposition, but he always recovers it at the decisive moment:

1	. . . .	K—B3!
2	P—B5	K—B2!
3	K—N5	K—N2!
4	P—B6ch	K—B2
5	K—B5	K—B1!

If 5 . . . K—N1?; 6 K—N6 wins. If 5 . . . K—K1?; 6K—K6 wins.

| 6 | K—K6 | K—K1 |
| 7 | P—B7ch | K—B1 |

8   K—B6   . . . .

Black is stalemated.

The Rook Pawn is a special case which leads to stalemate:

BLACK TO PLAY

1	. . . .	K—N1
2	K—N6	K—R1
3	P—R5	K—N1
4	P—R6	K—R1
5	P—R7	. . . .

Black is stalemated. If all the forces were one file to the left, this would be an easy win for White. But, as the position stands, Black's King has no escape at the side of the board, and stalemate is the consequence.

WHITE TO PLAY

A Rook Pawn (or any similar passed Pawn) can often win, however, when the hostile King is too far away to catch it. Take the position in the preceding diagram:

White wins by advancing his Pawn immediately:

1	P—R4	K—N1
2	P—R5	K—B1
3	P—R6	K—K1
4	P—R7	K—B1
5	P—R8/Qch and wins	

In the next position the power of a remote passed Pawn is illustrated indirectly:

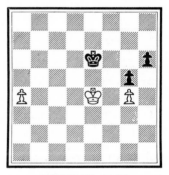

WHITE TO PLAY

1	P—R5	K—Q3
2	K—B5	K—B3

Black is able to stop the passed Pawn, but he cannot guard the King-side Pawns.

3	K—N6	K—N4
4	KxP	KxP
5	KxP and wins	

White will soon queen his remaining Pawn.

In the following game we have another example of a qualitatively superior Pawn:

WHITE TO PLAY

1 P—K6	K—B3

If 1 . . . P—N6; 2 P—K7, P—N7; 3 P—K8/Q, P—N8/Q; 4 Q—KN8ch, winning Black's Queen.

2	K—Q6	P—N6
3	P—K7	P—N7
4	P—K8/Q	P—N8/Q
5	Q—KB8ch	K—N4
6	Q—KN8ch and wins	

White wins the Queen after all!

Sometimes the necessity for obtaining the Opposition can lead to tricky sequences. Here is one example:

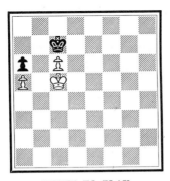

WHITE TO PLAY

This ending is much harder than it looks, for instance: 1 K—Q5, K—B1!; 2 K—Q6, K—Q1 and if 3 P—B7ch, K—B1; 4 K—B6, stalemate. The right way is:

1	K—Q5	K—B1!
2	K—Q4!	. . . .

2 K—B4! also wins.

2	. . . .	K—Q1
3	K—B4!	K—B1
4	K—Q5	. . . .

White's intentional loss of time has given him the right position for gaining the Opposition. If now 4 . . . K—Q1; 5 K—Q6, K—B1; 6 P—B7 and wins.

4	. . . .	K—B2
5	K—B5	
	and wins	

For now that White has the Opposition, Black's King must give way, allowing K—N6 which wins Black's remaining Pawn and thus allows White to win easily.

ENDINGS WITH MINOR PIECES

WHITE TO PLAY

As Black has no Pawns left, whatever winning chances there

are in this position are necessarily on White's side. The play demonstrates that the wide separation of White's Pawns gives the Bishop an impossible defense task.

1   P—R5   B—B1

Black has to be ready to play . . . B—B4 in answer to P—R6. Hence White's next move.

2   K—Q5   B—R3

So that if 3 P—R6, B—K6, etc.

3   P—N5ch!   . . . .

Beautiful play. If 3 . . . KxP; 4 P—R6 wins, as the Bishop is blocked off.

3   . . . .   BxP
4   K—K4!   . . . .

Prevents . . . B—K6.

4   . . . .   B—R5

In order to play . . . B—B7.

5   K—B3! and wins

Black cannot stop the Pawn from queening.

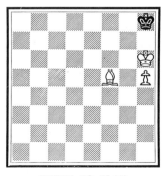

WHITE TO PLAY

The previous diagram illustrates a remarkable situation of fairly frequent occurrence. In this position the material advantage of a Bishop and Pawn is not enough to win.

(Actually it does not matter who moves first. White cannot force a win in any event.)

1	K—N6	K—N1
2	P—R6	K—R1

If now 3 P—R7 or B—K6 Black is stalemated. On other moves Black's King swings back and forth between King Rook 1 and King Knight 1 and no progress is made.

Another exceptional position appears in the following diagram:

WHITE TO PLAY

As a Knight cannot force checkmate, we would expect the ending to be drawn. Paradoxically, White can checkmate here because of Black's remaining Pawn.

1	N—N4ch	K—R8
2	K—B1	P—R7

The Pawn buries Black's King alive.

3	N—B2 mate

The following ending centers about White's attempt to queen

his Pawn. He is able to accomplish this thanks to the agility of
his Knight.

WHITE TO PLAY

1	N—B3	B—Q1
2	N—K5	K—R2
3	N—N4	K—R1

Or 3 . . . B—N4; 4 N—B6ch and the Pawn will queen.

4   N—B6! and wins

For if 4 . . . B—B2; 5 P—K7, etc.

Despite the fact that Black's forces are well placed for defense,
White can force the queening of his Pawn:

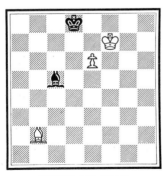

WHITE TO PLAY

1	B—B6ch	K—B1

If 1 . . . K—B2; 2 B—K7, B—Q5; 3 B—Q6ch!, KxB; 4 P—K7, and the Pawn queens.

2	B—K7	B—K6
3	B—N4	B—N4
4	B—B3!	B—Q1
5	B—B6!	BxB
6	KxB	K—Q1
7	K—B7!	
	and wins	

White forces the queening of his Pawn.

The following position is also won for White because he can draw off the Black Knight from the defense:

WHITE TO PLAY

1	N—N6	. . . .

This threatens to win at once because of the double threat 2 N—K5ch or 2 N—B8.

1	. . . .	K—Q4

The best defense. If instead 1 . . . K—B2; 2 N—B8, N—N1; 3 N—K6ch and wins. Or 1 . . . K—B4; 2 N—B8, N—K4!; 3 K—R8, N—B3; 4 N—K6ch, followed by 5 N—Q8.

	2 N—B8	N—K4!

For if 3 P—N8/Q?, N—B3ch draws.

3	K—N6	N—B3
4	N—Q7	K—Q3
5	N—K5!	N—N1
6	K—R7	K—B2
7	N—B4!	N—B3ch

If 7 . . . N—Q2; 8 N—N6, N—N1; 9 N—Q5ch and wins.

8	K—R8	N—N1!
9	N—N6!	N—R3

If 9 . . . N—B3; 10 N—Q5ch, followed by 11 N—N4, wins for White.

10	N—Q5ch	K moves
11	K—R7 and wins	

A material advantage is often insufficient to win where there are Bishops on opposite colors. This is the case in the following position:

WHITE TO PLAY

Black is able to draw, despite his minus of two Pawns, because the Pawns are only one file apart. This makes Black's defensive task fairly easy.

1	K—K6	B—N5
2	B—K4	K—Q1
3	K—B7	B—R6
4	P—K6	B—N5

White can make no headway.

In the next position White's Pawns are two files apart. This makes an impossibly wide defensive front for Black, and he cannot cover all threats.

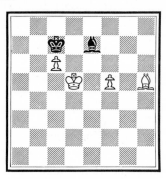

WHITE TO PLAY

1	B—B3	K—Q1
2	K—K6	B—N5
3	P—B6	B—R4
4	P—B7	B—N5
5	K—B6	B—B6ch
6	K—N6	B—N5

Or 6 . . . K—K2; 7 P—B7 winning at once.

7	K—N7 and wins

White wins the Bishop for one of the Pawns, and then queens the remaining Pawn.

ENDING WITH ROOKS

The classic winning position of Rook and Pawn *vs.* Rook appears in the following position:

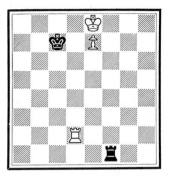

WHITE TO PLAY

The factors common to all examples of this ending are these: the Pawn is advanced to the seventh rank; the White King is in front of the Pawn; the Pawn is a Knight Pawn, Bishop Pawn, King Pawn, or Queen Pawn.

1   R—QB2ch   K—N2

If 1 . . . K—Q3?; 2 K—Q8 wins at once, as Black has no checks.

2   R—B4!   . . . .

To move the King at once is pointless: 2 K—Q7, R—Q8ch; 3 K—K6, R—K8ch; 4 K—Q6, R—Q8ch; 5 K—K5, R—K8ch, and White can make no progress because his King must stay near the Pawn or else move in front of it.

The idea of White's Rook move is to interpose eventually and thus break off the series of Black's Rook checks.

2	. . . .	R—B7
3	K—Q7	R—Q7ch
4	K—K6	R—K7ch
5	K—B6	R—KB7ch

If 5 . . . K—N3; 6 R—B8 wins at once. And if 5 . . . K—N1; 6 R—B5 to be followed by 7 R—K5 winning.

| 6 | K—K5 | R—K7ch |
| 7 | R—K4 | Resigns |

A Rook Pawn often fails to win; but here is an exceptional case where a Rook Pawn does win:

WHITE TO PLAY

| 1 | K—N5 | K—B2 |
| 2 | K—R6 | R—R1 |

If 2 . . . K—B3; 3 R—QB1ch, followed by 4 K—N7 and wins.

| 3 | R—QB1ch | K—Q3 |

If 3 . . . K—Q2; 4 K—N7 wins.

4	K—N7	R—R2ch
5	K—N8	R—R1ch
6	R—B8	Resigns

When the weaker side's forces are well placed, a draw is sometimes possible despite the Pawn minus. Here is an example:

Black's policy here is to keep his Rook on the third rank until White's Pawn reaches that rank. At that point Black's Rook goes to the eighth rank and checks wherever possible.

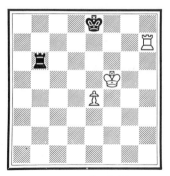

WHITE TO PLAY

1	P—K5	R—QR3
2	R—QN7	R—QB3
3	P—K6	R—B8!
4	K—B6	R—B8ch
5	K—K5	R—K8ch
6	K—Q6	R—Q6ch
	Draw	

Black's Rook keeps checking, and the only way for the King to escape the checks is to give up the Pawn.

BLACK TO PLAY

If it is Black's move in this position, he can draw because the White King cannot get back in time to win the Pawn.

Rook and minor piece *vs.* Rook is often no more than a draw. In the following diagram we have situations that favor the stronger side.

WHITE TO PLAY

1   B—B4!   . . . .

This threatens R—N8 mate, puts Black's Rook out of action, and prevents annoying Rook checks.

1   . . . .   K—B1
2   B—K6ch   K—Q1
3   R—N8ch   R—B1
4   RxR mate

BLACK TO PLAY

Positions in which a player has the Exchange ahead are almost always a win with Pawns on both sides. Where there are no Pawns on the Rook's side, the win can be quite difficult, if not impossible.

Black must be careful not to get trapped into a position where he is simultaneously threatened with mate and loss of the Bishop. Thus if 1 . . . B—K4; 2 R—K7 wins the Bishop. Also if 1 . . . B—R1; 2 R—QR7 wins at once.

	1	. . . .	B—N8
	2	R—B1	B—R7

If 2 . . . B—K6; 3 R—K1 wins. Other Bishop moves along the diagonal lose the same way.

	3	R—KR1	B—N6
	4	R—KN1	B—R7
	5	R—N2!	. . . .

Forces the Bishop onto one of the losing squares.

	5	. . . .	B—Q3
	6	R—Q2	B—K2

If 6 . . . B—B1; 7 R—Q8 and mate next move.

	7	R—QB2	B—R6
	8	R—B8ch	B—B1
	9	R—R8	Resigns

White mates next move.

When the player with the minor piece has a Pawn, the win is virtually impossible. In the following position, where Black has two Pawns, White can consider himself lucky to draw.

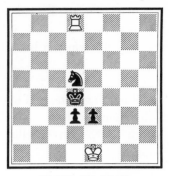

BLACK TO PLAY

1   . . . .   P—Q7ch

What stops Black from winning is that his King has little freedom of action. For example: 1 . . . K—K5; 2 R—K8ch, K—B6; 3 R—KB8ch, N—B5; 4 R—B7, P—Q7ch; 5 K—Q1, K—N6; 6 R—Q8 followed by 7 RxP and draws.

2	K—K2	K—B5
3	R—QB8ch	K—N6
4	R—Q8	N—B6ch
5	KxP	Drawn

White gives up his Rook for the remaining Pawn.

WHITE TO PLAY

In endings of Rook *vs.* Knight, the Knight must beware of getting too near the edge of the board. Once the Knight is driven to that sector, the chances of losing become very great.

Here the position of Black's pieces is extremely unfavorable.

1	R—K5!	N—R8ch

If 1 . . . K—R6; 2 R—K3 wins.

2	K—B3	N—N6

If 2 . . . K—N8; 3 R—K2, K—B1; 4 R—KN2 winning the Knight.

3	R—KN5	N—B8
4	K—B2	Resigns

White attacks the Knight and also threatens 5 R—KR5 mate.

QUEEN AND PAWN ENDINGS

This type of endgame requires a great deal of patience because of the Queen's enormous checking powers. Nevertheless, there are many winning possibilities which most players pass by.

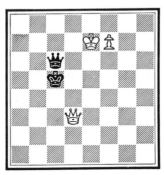

BLACK TO PLAY

1	. . . .	Q—B2ch

If 1 . . . Q—N2ch; 2 Q—Q7, Q—K5ch; 3 K—Q8 and wins. For Black cannot play 3 . . . Q—R1ch because of 4 Q—B8ch; nor can he play 3 . . . Q—KR5ch because of 4 Q—K7ch.

2	Q—Q7	Q—K4ch
3	K—Q8	Q—R1ch
4	Q—K8	Q—Q5ch
5	K—B8	Q—KN5ch
6	Q—Q7	. . . .

If now 6 . . . Q—B6, White wins by 7 Q—B7ch, K—Q5 (not 7 . . . K—Q4??; 8 Q—N7ch winning the Queen); 8 Q—Q6ch followed by 9 P—B8/Q.

6	. . . .	Q—N2
7	Q—K7ch	K—B3
8	P—B8/Q and wins	

WHITE TO PLAY

Here White has already reduced Black's checking possibilities to a minimum:

1	Q—K5ch	. . . .

And with this move he prevents Black's . . . Q—B5ch.

1	. . . .	K—N8
2	K—B7	Q—R2
3	Q—KN5!	K—N7
4	K—B8	Resigns

The Pawn must queen. (Another winning move for White is 4 Q—N6.)

Endings of Queen against Pawn are more common than we might expect. Sometimes they result from a queening race in which one Pawn queens while the opposing Pawn reaches the seventh rank. When the remaining Pawn is a Rook Pawn or Bishop Pawn and the stronger side's King is far away, the player with the Pawn has a good chance to draw. However, when the Pawn is a Knight Pawn, King Pawn, or Queen Pawn, the Queen wins, even when its supporting King is far away.

WHITE TO PLAY

In positions of this kind, the Queen has a standard winning procedure.

1	Q—KB5ch	K—N7

White's aim is to force Black's King in front of his Pawn.

2	Q—N4ch	K—B7
3	Q—B4ch	K—N7
4	Q—K3	K—B8
5	Q—KB3ch	K—K8

Now that the Pawn does not threaten to queen, White has time to bring his King to the scene of action.

6	K—B6	K—Q7
7	Q—B2	K—Q8

After 7 . . . K—Q6?; 8 Q—K1, Black's chances of a draw disappear at once.

8	Q—Q4ch	K—B7
9	Q—K3	K—Q8
10	Q—Q3ch	K—K8

Now White again wins time for the approach of his King.

11	K—Q5	K—B7
12	Q—Q2	K—B8
13	Q—B4ch	K—N7
14	Q—K3	K—B8
15	Q—KB3ch	K—K8
16	K—K4	. . . .

White's King will soon be able to co-operate in a checkmate.

16	. . . .	K—Q7
17	Q—Q3ch	K—K8
18	K—B3	K—B8
19	QxPch	K—N8
20	Q—KN2 mate	

Outstanding Chessmasters
and Their Memorable Games

Chess owes much to its World Champions and other great masters who have enriched the literature of the game with their many masterpieces. This section presents thumbnail sketches of the careers of twenty-four outstanding masters. In addition, each player is represented by one of his finest games.

ADOLF ANDERSSEN

ADOLF ANDERSSEN, born in Breslau, Germany, on July 6, 1818, died in 1879. Aside from his fame as a peerless combination player, Anderssen has the distinction of having won the first international tournament ever held (London, 1851).

From the time of Morphy's retirement (1859) until his defeat at the hands of Steinitz (1866), Anderssen was regarded as World Champion. His tournament victories at London (1862) and Baden-Baden (1870) showed that he always remained a master of the first rank. Anderssen's achievements were all the more remarkable since he was a schoolteacher and not a professional chessplayer.

Anderssen's games are always delightful to play over because of their highly imaginative character. He strives for attack at all cost, producing masterpieces of rare charm. "Attack! Always attack!" is Anderssen's motto.

Evans Gambit
Breslau, 1860

	WHITE A. Anderssen	BLACK Amateur			WHITE A. Anderssen	BLACK Amateur
1	P—K4	P—K4		6	Castles	P—Q3
2	N—KB3	N—QB3		7	P—Q4	PxP
3	B—B4	B—B4		8	PxP	B—N3
4	P—QN4	BxNP		9	P—Q5	N—R4
5	P—B3	B—B4		10	B—N2	. . . .

Threatening BxP. Anderssen's 9th move was played with a view to creating a magnificent diagonal for this Bishop.

10	. . . .	N—KB3	13	N—K2	Castles
11	B—Q3	B—N5	14	Q—Q2	R—B1
12	N—B3	P—B3	15	Q—N5	. . . .

Now Anderssen threatens to win a piece by BxN. This provokes the following exchange, giving White an open King Knight file which he turns to magnificent use.

15	. . . .	BxN	17	K—R1!	N—B5
16	PxB	PxP	18	R—KN1	N—K1

Black expects 19 BxP, when 19 . . . QxQ will let him off fairly lightly.

19	QxNPch!!	NxQ	21	R—N8 ch!!	KxR
20	RxNch	K—R1	22	R—N1ch	Q—N4
			23	RxQ mate	

A typical Anderssen attack.

PAUL MORPHY

PAUL MORPHY, who was born in New Orleans on June 22, 1837, and died in 1884, is considered by many the greatest of all the chessmasters. Though his formal career lasted only from 1857 to 1859, he accomplished enough in that short space of time to be regarded as the greatest player of his day.

After winning the American Championship in 1857, Morphy went to Europe, where he won matches by decisive scores against Loewenthal, Harrwitz, Owen, and Anderssen. He never played more than eight blindfold games in an exhibition, but the combination of dazzling brilliancy and meticulous accuracy made a profound impression on his contemporaries.

Morphy revolutionized chess with his insistence on rapid, purposeful development of the pieces. His masterpieces of sacrificial play are no mere swindles, and modern analysis has proved their general soundness. Though chess has undergone considerable development since Morphy's day, his games remain a lasting source of pleasure to students of later times.

Two Knights' Defense
New Orleans, 1858

	WHITE *P. Morphy*	BLACK *Amateur*		WHITE *P. Morphy*	BLACK *Amateur*
1	P—K4	P—K4	5	N—~N5	P—Q4!
2	N—KB3	N—QB3	6	PxP	NxP
3	B—B4	N—B3	7	Castles	B—K2
4	P—Q4	PxP	8	NxBP!	. . . .

Morphy sacrifices a piece to drive Black's King into the open.

| 8 . . . . | KxN | 10 N—B3!! | PxN |
| 9 Q—B3ch | K—K3 | 11 R—K1ch | N—K4 |

Having sacrificed a second piece, White continues with his proverbial elegance.

| 12 B—B4 | B—B3 | 13 BxN | BxB |

Now comes still another sacrifice that clinches the issue:

| 14 RxBch! | KxR | 15 R—K1ch | K—Q5 |
| | | 16 BxN | R—K1 |

If 16 . . . QxB; 17 QxP mate! After Black's last move, Morphy has a forced mate.

17 Q—Q3ch	K—B4	20 QxBPch	K—R5
18 P—QN4ch!	KxP	21 Q—-QN3ch	K—R4
19 Q—Q4ch	K—R4	22 Q—QR3ch	K—N3
		23 R—N1 mate	

This game has the authentic Morphy touch. He played it as one of six simultaneous blindfold games.

WILHELM STEINITZ

WILHELM STEINITZ, the first officially recognized World Champion, held the title from 1866 to 1894. He was born in Prague on May 14, 1836, and died in 1900.

The "modern school" owes its existence to Steinitz, who called attention to the importance of positional play and the dominating role played by a material advantage. Such was the powerful originality of Steinitz's ideas that the whole chess world divided into passionate admirers and equally fervent detractors of his theories.

In his many years of match play Steinitz rolled up a phenomenal record. His victims included Blackburne, Anderssen, Bird, Zukertort, Mackenzie, Tchigorin, and Gunsberg. His tournament record, though not quite so brilliant, shows many notable successes. Perhaps the outstanding one was first prize at Vienna, 1873, and his shared first prize at Vienna, 1882—two of the strongest tourneys of his generation.

Though Steinitz has often been condemned as the man who took the fun out of chess, he played many brilliant games. The game that follows is perhaps the most famous.

Giuoco Piano
Hastings, 1895

WHITE	BLACK		WHITE	BLACK
W. Steinitz	*C. Bardeleben*		*W. Steinitz*	*C. Bardeleben*
1 P—K4	P—K4	7	N—B3	P—Q4
2 N—KB3	N—QB3	8	PxP	KNxP
3 B—B4	B—B4	9	Castles	B—K3
4 P—B3	N—B3	10	B—KN5	B—K2
5 P—Q4	PxP	11	BxN	B/K3xB
6 PxP	B—N5ch	12	NxB	QxN

Steinitz plays for an open position, hoping to exploit Black's failure to castle. Black disregards the danger signals!

13 BxB	NxB	15 Q—K2	Q—Q2
14 R—K1	P—KB3	16 QR—B1	P—B3
		17 P—Q5!	. . . .

A Pawn sacrifice to open up the game.

17	PxP	19 N—K6	KR—QB1
18 N—Q4	K—B2	20 Q—N4	P—KN3

21   N—N5ch! K—K1

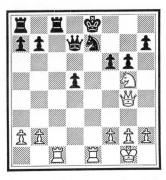

22   RxNch!!   K—B1

Steinitz has started a glorious combination. On 22 . . . QxR; 23 RxRch wins, and on 22 . . . KxR; 23 R—K1ch gives a winning attack.

With the threat of mate hanging over him, Steinitz nevertheless strikes home first:

23   R—B7ch!! K—N1   24   R—N7ch!! K—R1
                           25   RxPch!!   Resigns

For after 25 . . . K—N1; 26 R—N7ch!!, K—R1 White forces mate by 27 Q—R4ch!, KxR; 28 Q—R7ch, K—B1; 29 Q—R8ch, K—K2; 30 Q—N7ch, K—K1; 31 Q—N8ch, K—K2; 32 Q—B7ch, K—Q1; 33 Q—B8ch, Q—K1; 34 N—B7ch, K—Q2; 35 Q—Q6 mate! One of the most beautiful games in master play annals.

JOHANNES HERMAN ZUKERTORT

JOHANNES HERMAN ZUKERTORT was born in Lublin (Poland) on September 7, 1842, and died in London in 1888. He was Wilhelm Steinitz' greatest rival and a man of many gifts aside from his superb chess skill.

For example, Zukertort knew English, German, French, Spanish, and Italian, as well as Latin, Greek, Hebrew, Russian, Sanskrit, Arabic, and Turkish. He received nine medals for gallantry in the Prussian wars with Denmark, Austria, and France. He had a degree in medicine from the University of Breslau, though he never practiced. For many years Zukertort made a living as a journalist. He also excelled at dominoes, whist, fencing, and pistol-shooting.

That Zukertort also had time for chess seems hard to believe, but he was a first-rate master, a leading theoretician, an outstanding blindfold player, and one of the most unusual personalities the game has ever had. As a disciple of the great Anderssen, Zukertort acquired a taste for brilliant combinative play which characterized his whole subsequent career.

Queen's Gambit Declined
(By Transposition)
London, 1883

	WHITE J. H. Zuker-tort	BLACK J. H. Black-burne		WHITE J. H. Zuker-tort	BLACK J. H. Black-burne
1	P—QB4	P—K3	7	N—B3	Castles
2	P—K3	N—KB3	8	P—QN3	QN—Q2
3	N—KB3	P—QN3	9	B—N2	Q—K2
4	B—K2	B—N2	10	N—QN5!	N—K5
5	Castles	P—Q4	11	NxB	PxN
6	P—Q4	B—Q3	12	N—Q2	N/Q2—B3

After a close and cautious opening, Black has decided to operate on the Queen Bishop file to secure some compensation for White's two Bishops.

13	P—B3	NxN	17	QR—K1	R—B2
14	QxN	PxP	18	P—K4	QR—B1
15	BxP	P—Q4	19	P—K5	N—K1
16	B—Q3!	KR—B1	20	P—B4	P—N3

Zukertort has advanced powerfully in the center, and has the makings of a strong King-side attack. Blackburne still looks to the Queen Bishop file for counterplay.

21	R—K3!	P—B4	23	P—B5!	N—K5
22	PxP e.p.	NxP	24	BxN	PxB
			25	PxNP!!	R—B7

Blackburne has carried out his plan; but now he runs into a whole series of shocks.

| 26 | PxPch | K—R1 | 27 | P—Q5 dis ch | P—K4 |

Apparently White must lose a piece.

28   Q—N4!!!   R/B1—B4

If 28 . . . QxQ; 29 BxPch, KxP; 30 R—R3ch, K—N3; 31 R—N3ch, K—R3; 32 R—B6ch, K—R4; 33 R—B5ch, K—R3; 34 B—B4ch, K—R2; 35 R—R5 mate.

29   R—B8ch!!   KxP

If 29 . . . QxR; 30 BxPch, KxP; 31 QxPch, K—R3; 32 Q—R4ch, K—N3; 33 Q—N4ch, K—B2; 34 Q—K6 mate.

| 30 | QxPch | K—N2 | 32 | B—N7ch!! | K—N1 |
| 31 | BxPch!! | KxR | 33 | QxQ | Resigns |

JOSEPH HENRY BLACKBURNE

JOSEPH HENRY BLACKBURNE had a very long life and a correspondingly long career. Born in Manchester, England, on December 10, 1842, he died in 1924. His first international tournament was at London in 1862; his last at St. Petersburg in 1914.

Blackburne won many high prizes, his outstanding achievement being his first prize in the international tournament at Berlin, 1881. In match play he was less successful, and was overshadowed by the great Wilhelm Steinitz.

Famous above all for his brilliant attacking play, Blackburne was also a first-class endgame player. In addition, he distinguished himself as a blindfold expert and was one of the earliest celebrities in this field.

Center Game
Hastings, 1894

	WHITE Allies	BLACK J. H. Black- burne		WHITE Allies	BLACK J. H. Black- burne
1	P—K4	P—K4	6	N—QB3	KN—K2
2	P—Q4	PxP	7	Castles	Castles
3	QxP	N—QB3	8	P—B4?	P—Q4!
4	Q—K3	P—KN3	9	PxP	N—N5!
5	B—Q2	B—N2	10	B—B4	B—B4!

Beginning with his gain of time on move 3, Blackburne has developed very rapidly. He has already obtained a menacing attack.

11	B—N3	KNxP	13	Q—KB3	Q—B3!
12	NxN	NxN	14	P—B3	N—N5!

The Knight cannot be captured, and meanwhile Black threatens to win the White Queen by . . . N—Q6ch followed by a discovered check with the Knight.

	15	B—B4	Q—R3!!

If now 16 BxQ, NxP mate!

	16	P—N4	QxP!!

If now 17 BxQ, NxB mate; or 17 PxB, Q—R8 mate.

17   B—K3   BxBP!!

White resigns, as he is helpless against Black's three mating threats. (If 18 PxKB, Q—B7 mate.) A charming example of Blackburne's mastery of attacking play.

MICHAEL TCHIGORIN

MICHAEL TCHIGORIN, one of the greatest masters of the nineteenth century, was born in St. Petersburg on October 31, 1851, and died in 1908. Like Anderssen, Tchigorin was not a professional chessplayer, and spent most of his life as a minor official of the czarist regime.

Despite this, Tchigorin won many high prizes in international tournaments, his best achievement being his tie for first prize in the marathon tournament at New York in 1889. Tchigorin was also a superb match player, tying long matches with Tarrasch and Gunsberg and losing two World Championship matches to Steinitz by narrow margins.

Tchigorin was celebrated for the elegance of his keen attacking play, and he loved hazardous gambits above all. He frankly despised the "modern school" and its theories of positional chess. Yet Tchigorin was quite a theoretician himself and introduced some of the most interesting variations in the modern openings.

Through his beautiful games, theoretical investigations, and voluminous journalistic writings, Tchigorin founded a school of Russian chess that flourishes to this day.

Muzio Gambit
St. Petersburg, 1874

	WHITE M. Tchigorin	BLACK A. Davidov		WHITE M. Tchigorin	BLACK A. Davidov
1	P—K4	P—K4	8	P—Q3	B—R3
2	P—KB4	PxP	9	N—B3	N—K2
3	N—KB3	P—KN4	10	B—Q2	QN—B3
4	B—B4	P—N5	11	QR—K1	Q—KB4
5	Castles	PxN	12	N—Q5	K—Q1
6	QxP	Q—B3	13	B—B3	R—K1
7	P—K5!?	QxP	14	B—B6	. . . .

A popular variation in those far-off days. Black now manages to get rid of the troublesome pin, but Tchigorin has other unpleasant surprises in store for him.

14	. . . .	B—N4	17	P—KR4!	QxRP
15	P—KN4!	Q—N3	18	QxP	P—Q3
16	BxB	QxB	19	N—B6	N—K4

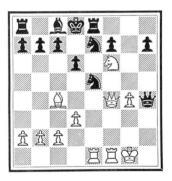

Black seems to be out of his troubles, but Tchigorin has prepared an exceptionally beautiful combination.

20	RxN!	PxR	21	QxP	BxP

If 21 . . . B—K3; 22 Q—Q4ch, K—B1; 23 BxBch, PxB; 24 Q—Q7ch forcing mate.

22 Q—Q4ch   K—B1   23 B—K6ch!!   K—N1

23 . . . BxB loses the Queen, while 23 . . . PxB leads to mate in three.

24 N—Q7ch   K—B1   26 N—R6ch!   PxN
25 N—B5 dis ch K—N1   27 Q—N4 mate

A perfect example of Tchigorin's dashing style.

DR. SIEGBERT TARRASCH

DR. SIEGBERT TARRASCH was born on March 5, 1862, in Breslau, and died in 1934. He established himself as one of the greatest masters of all time by an imposing series of tournament victories. But Tarrasch's memory is kept green not so much by his admittedly distinguished tournament successes as by a series of outstanding books in which he taught ordinary players the basic concepts of chess theory.

In an age when good chess books were scarce, Tarrasch hammered away at four basic principles:

1. Mobility is all-important.
2. Mobility confers the initiative.
3. Mobility creates its own plans.
4. Planning technique must be mastered.

We can instantly recognize Tarrasch's genius for teaching in this famous passage: "Chess is a form of intellectual productiveness; therein lies its peculiar charm. Intellectual productiveness is one of the greatest joys—if not the greatest one—of human existence. It is not everyone who can write a play, or build a bridge, or even make a good joke. But in chess everyone can, everyone must, be intellectually productive and so can share in this select delight. I have always a slight feeling of pity for the man who has no knowledge of chess, just as I would pity the man who has remained ignorant of love. Chess, like love, like music, has the power to make men happy."

Queen's Gambit Declined
St. Petersburg, 1914

WHITE	BLACK		WHITE	BLACK
A. Nimzo-	*Dr. S. Tar-*		*A. Nimzo-*	*Dr. S. Tar-*
vich	*rasch*		*vich*	*rasch*
1 P—Q4	P—Q4	6	Castles	B—Q3
2 N—KB3	P—QB4	7	P—QN3	Castles
3 P—B4	P—K3	8	B—N2	P—QN3
4 P—K3	N—KB3	9	QN—Q2	B—N2
5 B—Q3	N—B3	10	R—B1	Q—K2

White's opening lacks sting and leaves Black with a good game. In the phase that follows, Black actually takes the initiative.

11 BPxP?	KPxP	15	B—N5	N—K5!
12 N—R4	P—N3	16	BxN?	BxB
13 KN—B3	QR—Q1	17	Q—B2	NxN!
14 PxP	PxP	18	NxN	P—Q5!
		19	PxP?	BxPch!

Another brilliant example of the classic two-Bishop sacrifice which leaves White helpless.

20 KxB	Q—R5ch	21 K—N1	BxP!!

If now 22 KxB, Q—N5ch; 23 K—R1, R—Q4; 24 QxP, R—R4ch!; 25 QxR, QxQch; 26 . . . Q—N4ch winning the Knight.

22	P—B3	KR—K1!	25	P—Q5	P—B4!
23	N—K4	Q—R8ch	26	Q—B3	Q—N7ch
24	K—B2	BxR	27	K—K3	RxNch!

Black continues his brilliant attack with singular ferocity.

28	PxR	P—B5ch	30	K—K5	Q—R7ch
29	KxP	R—B1ch	31	K—K6	R—K1ch
			32	K—Q7	B—N4 mate

DR. EMANUEL LASKER

DR. EMANUEL LASKER, who was born in Berlin on December 24, 1868, won the World Championship in 1894 by winning a match from the titleholder, Wilhelm Steinitz. Thereafter Lasker reigned supreme until 1921, when he lost his title to Capablanca.

Lasker's style was by no means that of a perfectionist. He was above all a great fighter, often getting into critical situations and almost invariably escaping from them through sheer grit and resourcefulness. Even after losing his title, Lasker remained a power to be reckoned with, and as late as 1924, when he was 56, he won the great New York tournament ahead of Capablanca, Alekhine, Reti, Bogolyubov, and other younger men.

Lasker was no narrow specialist. He also achieved fame as a philosopher, mathematician, journalist, author, bridge master, and inventor of games.

Bird's Opening
Amsterdam, 1889

	WHITE	BLACK		WHITE	BLACK
	Dr. E. Lasker	*J. H. Bauer*		*Dr. E. Lasker*	*J. H. Bauer*
1	P—KB4	P—Q4	8	Castles	Castles
2	P—K3	N—KB3	9	N—K2	P—B4
3	P—QN3	P—K3	10	N—N3	Q—B2
4	B—N2	B—K2	11	N—K5	NxN
5	B—Q3	P—QN3	12	BxN	Q—B3
6	N—QB3	B—N2	13	Q—K2	P—QR3?
7	N—B3	QN—Q2	14	N—R5!	NxN

After this Black is helpless against White's brilliantly planned attack; if 14 . . . N—K1; 15 BxNP!, NxB; 16 Q—N4 and wins.

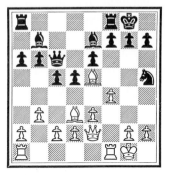

15	BxPch!!	KxB	19	R—B3	P—K4
16	QxNch	K—N1	20	R—R3ch	Q—R3
17	BxP!!	KxB	21	RxQch	KxR
18	Q—N4ch!	K—R2	22	Q—Q7!	. . . .

Only this move, which Lasker foresaw a long time ago, proves the soundness of his combination by winning a piece. Thereafter White wins by taking advantage of the exposed position of Black's King.

22	. . . .	B—KB3	28	P—K6	R—N2
23	QxB	K—N2	29	Q—N6	P—B3
24	R—KB1	QR—N1	30	RxPch!	BxR
25	Q—Q7	KR—Q1	31	QxBch	K—K1
26	Q—N4ch	K—B1	32	Q—R8ch	K—K2
27	PxP	B—N2	33	Q—N7ch	Resigns

This game will always be a classic of chess literature because of the masterly two-Bishop combination.

HARRY PILLSBURY

Harry Pillsbury was born in Somerville, Massachusetts, on December 5, 1872, and died in 1906. His tragically early death robbed the United States of its greatest player and a serious contender for World Championship honors.

As a virtual unknown, Pillsbury made chess history by winning the formidable Hastings tournament of 1895 ahead of Lasker, Steinitz, Tarrasch, Tchigorin, and other great masters. Of all of Lasker's contemporaries, Pillsbury proved to be the most dangerous adversary for the then World Champion.

Pillsbury's style was often brilliant and always characterized by hard fighting qualities that often wore down the opposition. His games are extremely attractive and deserve to be better known.

Queen's Gambit Declined
Hannover, 1902

	WHITE H. N. Pillsbury	BLACK R. Swiderski		WHITE H. N. Pillsbury	BLACK R. Swiderski
1	P—Q4	P—Q4	6	P—K4!	PxP
2	P—QB4	P—K3	7	N—K5	B—Q3
3	N—QB3	P—QN3?	8	Q—N4!	K—B1
4	N—B3	B—N2	9	B—QB4!	BxN
5	PxP	PxP	10	PxB	Q—Q5

Having forfeited the castling privilege, Black ought to avoid Pawn-grabbing expeditions with his Queen. This expedition, one must admit, is very tempting, but White has a keen refutation:

11   B—Q5!!   . . . .

If now 11 . . . BxB; 12 Q—B8ch, K—K2; 13 B—N5ch, P—B3; 14 R—Q1 and Black cannot stem the attack.

11	. . . .	P—QB3	13	B—B4	N—B3
12	BxKP	QxP	14	Q—R4!	Q—K2
			15	Castles (Q)!	. . . .

If now 15 . . . NxB?; 16 R—Q8ch wins the Queen.

15	. . . .	N—K1	18	B—Q5!	Q—B4
16	Q—N3!	N—R3	19	RxNch!	KxR
17	KR—K1	R—Q1	20	QxP	PxB

As a result of Pillsbury's vigorous play, the Black King is driven out into the open.

21	QxRch	K—Q2	25	Q—N8ch	R—Q1
22	QxP	K—B1	26	Q—N4ch	R—Q2
23	QxP!	P—Q5	27	B—K3!	BxP
24	Q—K6ch	R—Q2	28	RxP	Resigns

White must win a piece. This refreshing game is typical of Pillsbury's insouciant attacking style.

CARL SCHLECHTER

CARL SCHLECHTER, "the drawing master," was born in Vienna on March 2, 1874, and died in 1918. Of the 760 games he played in tournaments, he drew exactly 50 per cent, hence the nickname. Yet, as the following game shows, Schlechter was capable of unusually enterprising play and extraordinary brilliancy.

For over twenty years Schlechter consistently won high prizes, his outstanding successes being his first prizes at Ostend (1906) and Hamburg (1910). He also tied for first at Munich (1900) and Vienna and Prague (1908).

In match play Schlechter had a victory over Janowski and a drawn match with Tarrasch to his credit. But his greatest achievement of all was his 1910 tie-match with Emanuel Lasker for the World Championship. Though the rules governing the play enabled Lasker to retain his title, Schlechter was the only man who met him on even terms between 1894 and 1921.

Vienna Game
Cologne, 1898

WHITE	BLACK		WHITE	BLACK
C. Schlecht-	*W. Steinitz*		*C. Schlecht-*	*W. Steinitz*
er			*er*	
1 P—K4	P—K4	6 PxN	P—Q3
2 N—QB3	N—QB3	7 Castles	B—K3
3 B—B4	N—B3	8 P—QN3	P—B3
4 P—Q3	N—QR4	9 Q—Q3	B—K2
5 KN—K2!	NxB	10 B—N5	P—KR3

Chessplayers, like other people, do not always take their own advice. Steinitz, who always warned against weakening Pawn moves, has weakened his position with his 8th and 10th moves. Schlechter takes brilliant advantage of these faulty plays.

11 BxN!	BxB	12 QR—Q1	B—K2

With two Knights against two Bishops, Schlechter ought to be at a disadvantage. Far from being worried, he begins a brisk breakthrough:

13 P—B5!	PxP	15 QxNP	K—K2
14 Q—N3!	B—Q3	16 N—B4!!	. . . .

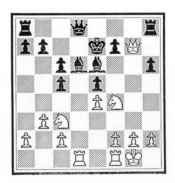

Schlechter's brilliant stroke does not leave Black much choice, for if 16 . . . PxN; 17 P—K5, BxKP; 18 QxB and Black's situation is bleak indeed.

16	. . . .	KR—N1		20	QxKPch	K—Q2
17	N—N6ch!	K—Q2		21	NxB!	QBPxN
18	RxBch!	KxR		22	RxPch	K—B3
19	R—Q1ch	B—Q4		23	N—K7ch	K—N3

Schlechter has engineered the whole attack with heartwarming verve. Now, instead of taking the Queen directly, he plays an even stronger move:

24 R—Q6ch!   Resigns

If 24 . . . K—B2; 25 R—KN6 dis ch leads to mate. Or if 24 . . . K—N4; 25 P—QR4ch, K—N5; 26 N—Q5ch, K—R6; 27 Q—R1 mate. A magnificent game!

FRANK JAMES MARSHALL

FRANK JAMES MARSHALL was born in New York City on August 10, 1877, and died in 1944. After becoming United States Champion in 1909, he retained the title until 1936, when he retired undefeated.

Though Marshall had some brilliant tournament triumphs (particularly at Cambridge Springs in 1904) he was an unpredictable player, at his best in an individual game. He was the most brilliant player of his generation, and his many masterpieces of attack have delighted chessplayers for many decades.

At the time of his death, *Chess Review* made this fitting comment: "There have been greater chessplayers than Frank Marshall, but none that loved the game more than he did. He gave to it a lifetime of devotion; not grudgingly, but with his whole heart, never regretting the choice. And his energies were not shared with any other occupation; all went for chess."

French Defense
Breslau, 1912

	WHITE S. Levitzky	BLACK *F. J. Mar-* *shall*		WHITE S. Levitzky	BLACK *F. J. Mar-* *shall*
1	P—Q4	P—K3	6	B—K2	N—B3
2	P—K4	P—Q4	7	Castles	B—K2
3	N—QB3	P—QB4	8	B—KN5	Castles
4	N—B3	N—QB3	9	PxP	B—K3
5	KPxP	KPxP	10	N—Q4	BxP

White has given his opponent an isolated Queen Pawn, but dissipates that positional advantage with his very next move. The result is that Black obtains active play for his pieces without any compensating drawback.

11	NxB	PxN	14	Q—Q2	B—N5!
12	B—N4	Q—Q3	15	BxN	RxB
13	B—R3	QR—K1	16	QR—Q1	Q—B4

Black's annoying pin provokes White into a clever simplifying continuation.

17	Q—K2	BxN	20	Q—R5	QR—KB1!
18	PxB	QxP	21	R—K5	R—R3
19	RxP	N—Q5!	22	Q—N5	RxB!

If now 23 PxR, N—B6ch winning White's Queen. So White tries another way.

23   R—QB5   Q—KN6!!!

Sometimes called "the most elegant move ever played in the history of chess." White resigned in the face of the following variations:

    I   24 BPxQ, N—K7ch and mate next move.

   II 24 BPxQ, N—K7 mate.

III   24 QxQ, N—K7ch; 25 K—R1, NxQch; 26 K—N1, NxR and
Black is a piece ahead.

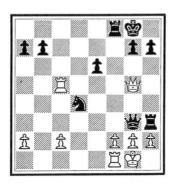

AKIBA RUBINSTEIN

AKIBA RUBINSTEIN (born in Stawiski, Russian Poland, on December 12, 1882) was probably the greatest of all the masters who failed to win the world title. In fact, due to lack of financial backing, Rubinstein never had a chance to play for the title.

He had, however, an imposing series of first prizes in tournaments. These included first in the great Carlsbad tournament of 1907, a tie for first with Ossip Bernstein in the big tournament at Ostende the same year, and a tie for first at St. Petersburg in 1909 with Emanuel Lasker, then World Champion. In this event Rubinstein had the satisfaction of winning a sensational game from Lasker.

In 1912 Rubinstein scored his most notable success by winning five first prizes, including those at Pistyan, Breslau (tie with Duras), and Vilna (Russian Championship). In later years he also won first prizes at Vienna (1922), Meran (1924), Marienbad (1925, tie with Nimzovich), and Rogaska-Slatina (1929).

Rubinstein was the great artist of the chessboard, capable of masterly combinations and subtle endgames. He rarely strayed from his beloved 1 P—Q4, deserting it occasionally for the King's Gambit. He was articulate only in his games; unlike some masters he contributed very little to the literature of chess.

Queen's Gambit Declined
Lodz, 1907

	WHITE	BLACK			WHITE	BLACK
	G. Rotlevi	*A. Rubinstein*			*G. Rotlevi*	*A. Rubinstein*
1	P—Q4	P—Q4		6	QPxP?	BxP
2	N—KB3	P—K3		7	P—QR3	P—QR3
3	P—K3	P—QB4		8	P—QN4	B—Q3
4	P—B4	N—QB3		9	B—N2	Castles
5	N—B3	N—B3		10	Q—Q2?	Q—K2!

White is playing inexact chess and allowing Black to gain the initiative.

11	B—Q3?	PxP!		16	NxN	BxN
12	BxBP	P—QN4		17	P—B4	B—B2
13	B—Q3	R—Q1		18	P—K4?	QR—B1
14	Q—K2	B—N2		19	P—K5	B—N3ch
15	Castles (K)	N—K4		20	K—R1	N—N5!

Further inexactitudes on White's part have given Rubinstein his chance. He follows up with one of the most brilliant attacks in the history of chess:

21	B—K4	Q—R5!		22	P—N3	. . . .

22	. . . .	RxN!!		24	QxR	BxBch
23	PxQ	R—Q7!!!		25	Q—N2	R—R6!!!

White resigns. The whole point of Rubinstein's deep combination is that White is helpless against the coming . . . RxP mate!

ARON NIMZOVICH

ARON NIMZOVICH was born in Riga on November 7, 1886, and died at the comparatively early age of 48 in 1935. Riga was famous for its strong chessplayers, and young Nimzovich became a player of master strength while still in his teens.

His strong bent for originality was obvious from the start, and before he was twenty he had worked out most of the details of his famous system. This was a co-ordinated body of chess doctrine involving such elements as the passed Pawn, blockade, the outpost, the Pawn chain, restraint, etc.

Though the chess world scoffed at Nimzovich's novel ideas, his list of high prizes was impressive, and for many years he was recognized as one of the world's greatest masters. There is no doubt that most of the masters developed since about 1925 have relied heavily on Nimzovich's concepts and have applied them consistently in their own games.

Queen's Indian Defense
Copenhagen, 1923

	WHITE F. Saemisch	BLACK A. Nimzovich		WHITE F. Saemisch	BLACK A. Nimzovich
1	P—Q4	N—KB3	6	N—B3	Castles
2	P—QB4	P—K3	7	Castles	P—Q4
3	N—KB3	P—QN3	8	N—K5	P—B3
4	P—KN3	B—N2	9	PxP	BPxP
5	B—N2	B—K2	10	B—B4	P—QR3!

Black's game is somewhat constricted and he therefore seizes the opportunity to expand on the Queen side.

11	R—B1	P—QN4	14	P—KR3	Q—Q2
12	Q—N3	N—B3	15	K--R2	N—R4!
13	NxN	BxN	16	B—Q2	P—B4!

17	Q—Q1	P—N5!	19	R—N1	B—Q3!
18	N—N1	B—QN4	20	P—K4	. . . .

Apparently decisive, as 20 . . . N—B3? is refuted by 21 P—K5 and 20 . . . P—N3 by 21 PxQP. But Nimzovich has deliberately provoked this strong-looking move. The following sacrifice of a piece is particularly subtle.

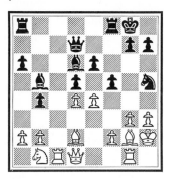

20	. . . .	BPxP!	23	K—R1	R/B1—B4!
21	QxN	RxP	24	Q—K3	B—Q6!
22	Q—N5	QR—KB1	25	QR—K1	P—R3!!!

White resigns, as he cannot find any move worth playing, for example:

    I   26 B—QB1, BxN and Black has won back the piece, remaining two Pawns ahead.

    II   26 QR moves, R—K7 winning the Queen.

    III   26 KR moves, BxR with an easy win.

    IV   26 B—KB1 or K—R2, R/B4—B6 winning the Queen.

    V   26 P—N4, R/B4—B6; 27 BxR, R—R7 mate!

JOSÉ RAOUL CAPABLANCA

JOSÉ RAOUL CAPABLANCA .was born in Havana on November, 19, 1888, and died in New York in 1942. After learning the moves at the age of four, he showed great aptitude for the game, becoming Champion of Cuba at the age of twelve. In 1909 he established himself as one of the world's leading masters without ever having played in a master tournament. He accomplished this feat by vanquishing Frank Marshall, the American Champion, by 8–1, only two years after Marshall had made a futile try to wrest the World Championship from Emanuel Lasker.

Going on from one triumph to another, Capablanca finally became World Champion in 1921 by winning a title match from Emanuel Lasker. Thereafter Capablanca disappointed his admirers by holding on to the title for only six years.

Capablanca's style was the very essence of simplicity and forcefulness. Though he disliked complications, he was a very fine tactician. His special domain was the endgame, which he played with much-admired precision and clarity. At his best, Capablanca was a chess artist of very fine sensibilities.

Dutch Defense
(By Transposition)
Havana, 1912

WHITE	BLACK		WHITE	BLACK
J. R. Capablanca	*Amateur*		*J. R. Capablanca*	*Amateur*
1 P—Q4	P—Q4	6	P—B4	Q—B3
2 P—K3	P—K3	7	P—QN3	N—KR3
3 B—Q3	P—QB3	8	B—N2	Castles
4 N—KB3	B—Q3	9	Q—B2	N—Q2
5 QN—Q2	P—KB4	10	P—KR3!	P—KN3

Black rightly fears White's threatened P—KN4. The text parries that threat, but it creates a weakness on the long diagonal which Capablanca exploits in superb style.

11	Castles (Q)	P—K4?	13	PxP	PxP
12	QPxP	NxP	14	N—B4!!	. . . .

A lightning flash in a clear sky. This is the first of a series of beautiful sacrifices.

14	. . . .	PxN		17	NxN	B—K3
15	BxPch	N/R3—B2		18	R—Q1	Q—K2
16	RxB!!	QxR		19	R—Q7!!	BxR
				20	NxB	. . . .

If now 20 . . . QxN; 21 Q—B3! wins. This is the point of White's previous sacrifices.

20 . . . .   KR—B1

Black plays to give his King some room and to get rid of one of the terrible Bishops.

21	Q—B3!	RxB		22	PxR	Resigns

For after 22 . . . N—Q3; 23 Q—R8ch is deadly.

EVIM BOGOLYUBOV

Evim Bogolyubov was born near Kiev (Russian Ukraine) on April 14, 1889, and died in 1952. Though his career was overshadowed by that of his great countryman Alekhine, Bogolyubov was recognized as one of the strongest masters of modern times.

Two attempts to wrest the world title from Alekhine in 1929 and 1934 both failed. Yet Bogolyubov's many successes in outstanding tournaments left the chess world in no doubt about his abilities.

Bogolyubov was primarily a master of attack. His play was

often extraordinarily brilliant, and always aggressive. His opti-
mistic fighting temperament carried him instinctively through
many far-reaching combinations beyond the grasp of most
players.

The following game is especially interesting because it was
played during his internment in Germany during World War I—
the period in which he developed from a fair player into a grand-
master.

Ruy Lopez
Baden-Baden, 1914

WHITE	BLACK		WHITE	BLACK
A. Flamberg	E. Bogolyubov		A. Flamberg	E. Bogolyubov
1 P—K4	P—K4	4	B—R4	N—B3
2 N—KB3	N—QB3	5	P—Q4	NxKP
3 B—N5	P—QR3	6	Castles	P—QN4
		7	NxP	. . . .

Complications have set in at a remarkably early stage. If now
7 . . . PxB; 8 NxN, PxN; 9 R—K1 and White wins back the
piece.

7	NxN	8 PxN	P—Q4

And here 8 . . . PxB can be met by 9 Q—Q5.

9 PxP e.p.	BxP	10 B—N3	. . . .

The apparently formidable 10 R—K1 holds no terrors for Black,
who simply plays 10 . . . Castles! and if 11 RxN??, BxPch winning the Queen.

10	B—N2	12 PxP	Q—R5
11 P—QR4	Castles	13 P—R3	NxP!

The first of a series of forceful and imaginative moves which
eventually leave White helpless.

14	RxN	B—B4	15	Q—B1	QR—K1

With the murderous threat of 16 . . . BxRch; 17 QxB, R—K8ch and wins.

16	B—Q2	R—K4	18	PxP	BxRP!
17	R—R4	Q—K2	19	QxB	. . . .

If 19 RxB, R—K7 is very strong.

19	. . . .	R—K8ch!	21	N—B3	Q—K4ch
20	K—R2	BxR	22	R—B4	. . . .

On 22 B—B4 Black has a surprise mate starting with . . . R—R8ch!

22	. . . .	P—N4	25	BxB	PxBch
23	Q—N5	PxR	26	K—N1	Q—K6ch
24	BxR	B—N6ch	27	K—R1	Q—K8ch

White resigns, as it is mate next move.

RICHARD RETI

RICHARD RETI was born on May 18, 1889, near Bratislava, then located in Hungary and later a part of Czechoslovakia. He died in 1929.

Together with Nimzovich and Alekhine, Reti was famous in the 1920's as one of the chief "Hypermodern" masters. He had a remarkably scholarly grasp of the development of chess theory and therefore, despite his "modernistic" tendencies, a deep appreciation of the nineteenth-century masters.

Reti was one of the few players of modern times to have an opening named after him: Reti's Opening. It embodies a wealth of subtle details that call for a very fine understanding of the principles of position play.

While Reti was one of the most successful masters of his day, he is best remembered for his many beautiful games and his artistic endgame compositions.

Reti's Opening
New York, 1924

WHITE	BLACK	WHITE	BLACK
R. Reti	E. Bogolyubov	R. Reti	E. Bogolyubov
1 N—KB3	N—KB3	7 B—N2	QN—Q2
2 P—B4	P—K3	8 P—Q4	P—B3
3 P—KN3	P—Q4	9 QN—Q2	N—K5?
4 B—N2	B—Q3	10 NxN!	PxN
5 Castles	Castles	11 N—K5	P—KB4
6 P—N3	R—K1	12 P—B3!	. . . .

With this move, which forces open valuable lines for White, he refutes Black's faulty ninth move.

12	PxP	14 NxN	BxN
13 BxP	Q—B2	15 P—K4	P—K4!?

Black fights hard for his shares of the vital center, and White must play very well to demonstrate an advantage.

16 P—B5	B—KB1	20 BxP	RxKBP
17 Q—B2	PxQP	21 RxR	BxR
18 PxP	QR—Q1	22 QxB	RxB
19 B—R5	R—K4	23 R—KB1	R—Q1

Black has fought hard to equalize, but without quite succeeding, as Reti now brilliantly proves:

24 B—B7ch!   K—R1   25 B—K8!!   Resigns

No matter how Black struggles, he must lose a piece. If 25 . . . RxB; 26 QxBch forces mate. If 25 . . . BxPch; 26 QxB and the Bishop is still immune. And if 25 . . . B—K2; 26 Q—B8ch!, BxQ; 27 RxB mate. The utter simplicity of White's play in this game is perhaps even more pleasing than flashy brilliancy.

ALEXANDER ALEKHINE

ALEXANDER ALEKHINE, the greatest player of modern times and perhaps of all time, was born in Moscow on November 1, 1892, and died in Lisbon in 1946.

About Alekhine's pre-eminence as an attacking player there can be no doubt. One of his chief rivals, Max Euwe, once remarked of Alekhine: "He is a poet who creates a work of art out of something which would hardly inspire another man to send home a picture postcard." Alekhine's magnificent imaginative gifts also enabled him to hold the world record in blindfold play for many years.

Alekhine became World Champion in 1927 by defeating the titleholder, J. R. Capablanca. In 1935 Alekhine lost the title to Max Euwe, but regained it two years later in a return match. Alekhine held the title until his death in 1946. During his tenure he defeated Bogolyubov twice in challenge matches for the title.

In tournament play Alekhine also had many notable successes

to his credit, the outstanding ones being his first prizes at Baden-Baden, 1925; San Remo, 1930; and Bled, 1931.

French Defense
Tarnopol, 1916 (blindfold game)

WHITE	BLACK		WHITE	BLACK
A. Alekhine	*M. Feldt*		*A. Alekhine*	*M. Feldt*
1 P—K4	P—K3	5	N—K4	P—KB4?
2 P—Q4	P—Q4	6	N—N5!	B—K2
3 N—QB3	N—KB3	7	N/N5—B3	P—B3
4 PxP	NxP	8	N—K5	Castles

Alekhine has posted a Knight powerfully on the "hole" at King 5 created by Black's weakening 5th move. His method of turning this weakness to account is very impressive.

9 N/N1—B3	P—QN3	12	P—B4	N—B3
10 B—Q3	B—N2	13	B—B4	QN—Q2
11 Castles	R—K1	14	Q—K2	P—B4

He had apparently freed himself; but now Alekhine smashes his flimsy position to bits.

15 N—B7!!!	KxN	16	QxPch!!	K—N3

Or 16 . . . KxQ; 17 N—N5 mate!

17 P—KN4!	B—K5	18	N—R4 mate

One of the most beautiful masterpieces ever produced on the chessboard!

DR. MAX EUWE

DR. MAX EUWE, who was born at Watergraafsmeer, Holland, on May 20, 1901, became World Champion by defeating Alexander Alekhine in an exciting match played in 1935.

Although Euwe lost the title back to Alekhine only two years later, his 1935 victory firmly established his major position in chess history.

In his earlier years, Euwe achieved a reputation by a series of closely contested matches with some of the world's leading masters. A schoolteacher by profession, Euwe had only a limited amount of time available for training and serious play. Despite this handicap he was able to win the world title.

Aside from producing many fine games, Euwe has served the chess world well in other respects. He has written many excellent works on the game, and he has thereby contributed enormously to the popularity of chess. This has been particularly true of his native land, which has organized many large-scale tournaments and has produced a number of very strong players.

Giuoco Piano
Maastricht, 1946

	WHITE T. van Scheltinga	BLACK Dr. M. Euwe		WHITE T. van Scheltinga	BLACK Dr. M. Euwe
1	P—K4	P—K4	6	P—Q4	Q—K2
2	N—KB3	N—QB3	7	P—QR4	P—QR3
3	B—B4	B—B4	8	P—R3	N—B3
4	P—B3	P—Q3	9	R—K1	Castles
5	Castles	B—N3	10	P—QN4	K—R1

Black's formation is solid but somewhat on the conservative side. This provokes White into premature aggression.

11	B—R3	N—KN1!	14	BxN	BPxN!
12	P—N5	N—R4!	15	B—R2	KPxP
13	NxP?	P—KB3!!	16	N—Q2	BxP!

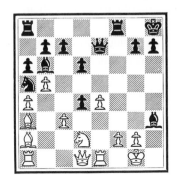

Black's last move shows White the error of his ways, for if 17 PxB, Q—N4ch; 18 K—B1, RxPch!; 19 KxR, P—Q6 dis ch, and Black has a crushing attack.

| 17 | N—B3 | B—N5 | 19 | Q—Q3 | BxN |
| 18 | BPxP | PxP | 20 | PxB | . . . . |

Now it is White who is on the defensive!

| 20 | . . . . | Q—N4ch | 22 | B—B1 | Q—R4 |
| 21 | K—B1 | N—B5! | 23 | PxP | RxP!! |

For if 24 QxN, Black wins with 24 . . . R—KR6!

| 24 | BxN | RxR! | 25 | Q—Q1 | RxB! |

White resigns, as 26 QxR/B1 is refuted by 26 . . . R—KR6! Black's breezy play is refreshing.

MIGUEL NAJDORF

MIGUEL NAJDORF was born in Warsaw on April 10, 1910. At the outbreak of World War II he found himself in Buenos Aires and has resided in that city since then.

Najdorf is one of the strongest living masters and has won

many high prizes in the most famous tournaments of modern times. He lost both of his matches against Reshevsky, but by impressively narrow margins.

Najdorf is capable of remarkably brilliant chess, and is noted for his imaginative, resourceful style. Though somewhat lacking in patience, he handles difficult positions with a richness of ideas that few other masters can equal.

Najdorf has twice broken the world's blindfold record, and his achievement of 45 games blindfold games played simultaneously is one which may defy competition for years to come.

French Defense
Lodz, 1929

	WHITE M. Najdorf	BLACK A. Sapiro		WHITE M. Najdorf	BLACK A. Sapiro
1	P—K4	P—K3	4	NxP	N—Q2
2	P—Q4	P—Q4	5	N—KB3	KN—B3
3	N—QB3	PxP	6	B—Q3	B—K2

The variation selected by Black has a bad reputation because it is too passive.

7	Castles	P—QN3?	9	NxNch	PxN?
8	N—K5!	B—N2	10	NxP!!	. . . .

A very fine sacrifice "on spec." White relies on his vastly superior development and the lasting pressure that results from it.

10	. . . .	KxN	14	B—QB4	Q—Q3
11	Q—R5ch	K—N1	15	B—KR6	B—KB1
12	R—K1	N—B1	16	R—K1	B—B1
13	RxP!!	NxR	17	Q—K8!	B—Q2

White now winds up the game with a scintillating combination worthy of what has gone on so far.

18	RxN!!		RxQ		20	BxBch		QxB
19	RxR dis ch		B—K3		21	RxB mate		

One of the most brilliant games ever played.

SAMUEL RESHEVSKY

Samuel Reshevsky was born on November 26, 1911, in Ozorkov (Russian Poland) and lives in the United States. He learned to play chess when he was four years old; by the time he was six, he was giving simultaneous exhibitions. Extensive tours of Europe and the United States made him world famous.

Retiring at an early age, Reshevsky resumed his chess career in 1931, and soon made good the promise of his early years. He won the United States Championship in 1936, and has been known since that time as the strongest American player.

Reshevsky's successes are based above all on his remarkable grit and tenacity. Though he is often in great time pressure, he can play "rapid transit" with phenomenal skill. Over the years his style has mellowed, so that many of his games are masterpieces of logical and forceful play.

French Defense
U. S. Open Championship, 1944

	WHITE S. Reshevsky	BLACK A. Vascon- cellos		WHITE S. Reshevsky	BLACK A. Vascon- cellos
1	P—K4	P—K3	7	Castles	N—QB3
2	P—Q4	P—Q4	8	B—KB4	Q—B2
3	P—K5	P—QB4	9	N—B3	P—QR3
4	PxP	N—Q2	10	R—K1	Q—N3?
5	N—KB3	BxP	11	B—N3	QxP?
6	B—Q3	N—K2	12	NxP!!	. . . .

Emboldened by Black's time-losing Queen moves, Reshevsky decides on a speculative sacrifice which leads to interesting play.

12	. . . .	PxN	15	PxPch	KxP
13	R—N1!	Q—R6	16	B—R4	N—QN5?
14	P—K6!	N—B3	17	N—K5ch	K—B1
			18	BxN	NxB

White is now ready for an unusually brilliant finish which at one point leaves all his pieces *en prise!*

19	BxPch!	KxB	22	Q—N5ch	K—R1
20	RxPch!!	B—K2	23	N—N6ch!	PxN
21	Q—R5!	R—B1	24	Q—R6ch	K—N1

25 QxPch   K—R1   26 R/N7xB   Resigns

Mate is unavoidable. One of those brilliant games that demonstrate the ability of the modern master to produce dashing chess when given the opportunity by his opponent.

MIKHAIL BOTVINNIK

MIKHAIL BOTVINNIK was born in St. Petersburg on August 17, 1911, and won the World Championship in 1948. He was the first Champion to win his title in a qualifying tournament rather than in a match with the reigning Champion. This was possible because the death of Alexander Alekhine in 1946 left the chess world without a titleholder.

Botvinnik's style owes much to Alekhine and Nimzovich. His opening repertoire is severely limited but resourceful, devoted to lines of play that confront both players with taxing problems. Subtle maneuvering is Botvinnik's forte, but, as becomes a World Champion, he is a thorough master of all departments of the game.

In the middle game Botvinnik does not strive for brilliancy so much as for depth of conception. When the position is ripe for combinations, however, Botvinnik reveals himself as an unsurpassed master of tactics. In the endgame, too, Botvinnik knows how to reduce complicated lines to crystal clarity. Above all, Botvinnik excels in rising to the occasion when the situation becomes particularly trying. This fighting quality Botvinnik demonstrated to perfection by tying Bronstein (1951) and Smyslov (1954) in hard-fought matches to retain his title.

Sicilian Defense
Nottingham, 1936

WHITE	BLACK		WHITE	BLACK
A. Alekhine	*M. Botvinnik*		*A. Alekhine*	*M. Botvinnik*
1 P—K4	P—QB4	3	P—Q4	PxP
2 N—KB3	P—Q3	4	NxP	N—KB3

5	N—QB3	P—KN3	8	N—N3	B—K3
6	B—K2	B—N2	9	P—B4	Castles
7	B—K3	N—B3	10	P—N4!	P—Q4!

White is making a determined effort to overrun Black's position. Only an alert defense can maintain the position for Black. Realizing this, he sacrifices a Pawn to maintain his freedom.

| 11 | P—B5! | B—B1 | 13 | P—Q6! | QxP! |
| 12 | KPxP | N—N5 | 14 | B—B5! | . . . . |

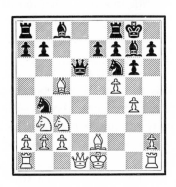

If Black tries to simplify, he loses: 14 . . . QxQch?; 15 RxQ, NxBPch?; 16 K—Q2 winning the Knight.

Or if (after 14 . . . QxQch?; 15 RxQ) Black tries 15 . . . N—B3 there follows 16 P—N5, N—Q2; 17 P—B6 and Black's game is hopeless.

Well aware of these dangers, Black fights back magnificently to achieve a draw.

| 14 | . . . . | Q—B5!! | 16 | BxN | NxP! |
| 15 | R—KB1 | QxRP | 17 | BxN | Q—N6ch |

Now White must not move his King and a perpetual check is in order.

| 18 | R—B2 | Q—N8ch |

Now White has nothing better than 19 R—B1, Q—N6ch, etc.

The game was therefore abandoned as a draw. A masterpiece of virile fighting chess.

PAUL KERES

PAUL KERES was born on January 7, 1916, in Narva (Estonia). As a very young player he made a reputation for himself for brilliancy second only to Morphy's. After distinguishing himself in the Warsaw Team Tournament of 1935, he rose to a pre-eminent position in only three years by tying with Reuben Fine for first prize in the great AVRO Tournament of 1938.

Since the end of World War II Keres has been a Soviet master and has won the U.S.S.R. Championship. Though he remains one of the world's best players, he has not quite fulfilled the promise of his earlier years. His dashing style is still in evidence, though somewhat chastened by experience and study.

King's Indian Defense
Ostend, 1937

WHITE	BLACK		WHITE	BLACK
A. Dunkelblum	*P. Keres*		*A. Dunkelblum*	*P. Keres*
1 P—Q4	N—KB3	5	Castles	Castles
2 N—KB3	P—B4	6	P—B4	P—Q4
3 P—K3	P—KN3	7	BPxP	NxP
4 B—K2	B—N2	8	PxF	N—R3!?

After an excessively quiet opening, Keres is determined to stir up complications.

9 BxN	PxB	14 B—R5	Q—B3
10 N—Q4	Q—B2	15 BxR	B—QR3!
11 N—N3	R—Q1	16 N—R5!	Q—K3!
12 Q—K2	P—QR4!	17 Q—Q2	BxR
13 B—Q2	P—R5!	18 N—B3	BxP!

At the cost of some material, Keres has conjured up a wild position very much to his taste.

| 19 | KxB | RxB | 20 | K—R1 | P—R6! |

If now 21 NxN, Q—K5ch; 22 P—B3, RxN!; 23 Q—KB2, PxP! and wins.

| 21 | R—Q1 | PxP! | 22 | NxN | RxN! |

White resigns, for after 23 Q—B2, RxRch; 24 QxR, Q—K5ch; 25 P—B3, P—N8/Q, Black is a Queen to the good!

VASSILY SMYSLOV

Vassily Smyslov, who was born in Moscow on March 23, 1921, is one of the strongest Russian players. Smyslov began winning master tournaments while still in his teens and has been a consistently high scorer since then.

In the Candidates' Tournament of 1948 Smyslov came second to Botvinnik, ahead of Keres and Reshevsky. In the 1953 Candidates' Tournament at Zurich he took first prize in convincing style. This earned him the right to play Botvinnik in 1954 for the World Championship, and after a very exciting struggle the match ended in a tie. Thus Smyslov lost his chance for the title by the narrowest of margins.

Originally a very brilliant player, Smyslov has come to rely more and more on positional methods. However, he remains a dangerous tactician, and he undoubtedly owes much of his success to his cold-blooded resourcefulness in trying situations.

Sicilian Defense
Groningen, 1946

	WHITE	BLACK		WHITE	BLACK
	V. Smyslov	C. Kottnauer		V. Smyslov	C. Kottnauer
1	P—K4	P—QB4	5	N—QB3	P—QR3
2	N—KB3	P—Q3	6	B—K2	P—K3
3	P—Q4	PxP	7	Castles	P—QN4?
4	NxP	N—KB3	8	B—B3!	R—R2

Black's 7th move looks suspiciously premature. White exploits
it with great energy.

9	Q—K2	R—B2	11	P—QR4!	PxP
10	R—Q1	QN—Q2	12	NxRP	B—N2

White is now ready for a decisive assault.

13	P—K5!	NxP	16	N—B6!	NxN
14	BxB	RxB	17	QxNch	N—Q2
15	QxP	Q—N1	18	N—B5!!	. . . .

This brilliant sacrifice must be accepted, for if 18 . . . R—B2;
19 NxN, RxN; 20 R—R8 wins the Queen.

18	. . . .	PxN	19	B—B4!!	B—Q3

If 19 . . . QxB; 20 Q—B8ch, K—K2; 21 QxR, and Black is
helpless.

20	BxB	R—N3	21	QxNch!	Resigns

A pretty finishing touch. After 21 . . . KxQ; 22 BxQ dis ch, White is a piece to the good. A very attractive game, played by White with smooth power and gusto.

DAVID BRONSTEIN

DAVID BRONSTEIN, who was born at Belaya Tserkov (Russia) on February 19, 1924, is the youngest contemporary master of World Championship caliber. He is also the most daring of present-day masters. Bronstein thinks nothing of playing the King's Gambit against formidable opponents, and he readily turns any opening into a gambit. In fact, at any stage of the game he is ready to sacrifice material for purely speculative reasons.

To play this type of fighting chess is not easy; to play against it is also not easy! Bronstein's fighting style makes him a greatly feared opponent. His hard-fighting style creates difficulties for himself and for his opponent as well.

Bronstein made his mark in international chess by winning the Interzonal Tournament at Saltsjobaden (Sweden) in 1948. This qualified him for the World Championship Candidates' Qualifying Tournament held at Budapest two years later. Here Bronstein, playing superb fighting chess, tied for first prize with his countryman Boleslavsky. Later in the year Bronstein defeated Boleslavsky by a one-point margin in a bitterly contested match. In 1951, having earned the right to play Botvinnik for the World Championship, Bronstein came within an ace of winning the title by drawing the match after leading a good part of the way.

Nimzoindian Defense
Budapest, 1950

	WHITE	BLACK		WHITE	BLACK
	D. Bronstein	*M. Najdorf*		*D. Bronstein*	*M. Najdorf*
1	P—Q4	N—KB3	4	P—K3	Castles
2	P—QB4	P—K3	5	P—QR3	BxNch
3	N—QB3	B—N5	6	PxB	P—Q3

White wants open lines for his Bishops; Black should strive for a blocked position.

7	B—Q3	P—B4	10	Castles	P—QN3
8	N—K2	N—B3	11	P—B4	B—R3?
9	P—K4	N—K1!	12	P—B5!	P—K4

Black thinks he has blocked the position, but White has a dynamic resource.

13   P—B6!!   K—R1

Or 13 . . . NxBP; 14 B—N5, leading to much the same kind of play.

14	P—Q5	N—R4	17	Q—R5	BxN
15	N—N3!	PxP	18	PxB	KR—N1
16	N—B5	B—B1	19	R—B3!	. . . .

Threatens mate in four moves, beginning with 20 QxRPch!!

| 19 | . . . . | R—N2 | 21 | R—R3 | N—KN2 |
| 20 | B—R6 | R—KN1 | 22 | Q—R4! | Resigns |

There is nothing to be done against the threat of 23 B—N5!, P—R4; 24 QxPch!!, NxQ; 25 RxNch, K—N2; 26 B—R6ch and mate follows. The game is noteworthy because of White's energetic and quickly decisive King-side attack.

Blindfold Chess

There are 318,979,654,000 ways to play the first four moves in a game of chess. By the time we get to the problem of how many different ways to play the first *ten* moves, the number has risen to the staggering figure of 169,518,829,100,544,000,000,-000,000,000!

Yet for at least eight hundred years there have been experts who could play chess blindfold. During the Golden Age of Saracen chess in the Middle Ages there were a number of chess-players who were able to conduct several games blindfold. Buzeccia, perhaps the greatest of Arab masters, visited Florence, Italy, in 1266 and played three of the outstanding Italian players simultaneously—two of them blindfold.

Of course, "blindfold" players aren't actually blindfolded when they give an exhibition. They sit with their back to the games, calling out their moves, which are made for them on each board; then their opponents make their replies, each calling out a move in turn. This process is of course made possible by the chess notation, which gives every square on the board a distinctive name.

Blindfold chess requires a combination of several remarkable qualities. The most obvious is a vivid imagination; right at the start, a player must be able to visualize the 32 men as they are placed on the 64 squares. From then on he must keep track of the changes, some of them far reaching, that occur from move to move.

The blindfold player must have a tenacious, infallible memory. If one little detail is "blacked out," the whole mental picture of the game is spoiled. He must have the ability to concentrate: let his attention wander for a while, and anything may come into his mind instead of that chessboard with its numerous pieces jumbled "haphazardly" in every sector.

To play two or more games blindfold simultaneously is surely one of the most phenomenal mental feats in the history of mankind; in fact, when the great Philidor managed to play three games simultaneously in 1782, the newspapers raved, affidavits were prepared, chessplayers and laymen marveled. Yet the modern chessmasters have steadily increased number of games played blindfold simultaneously until the record now stands at 45.

Let us be clear about what such a stupendous feat involves. Assume a player is conducting a single game blindfold. If he "sees" all the board and chessmen as one composite image at any given point, and the game goes 35 moves, that means that while the game is in progress, he must "see"—and remember perfectly! —70 such images. Now if he plays 30 games simultaneously, and we again assume 35 moves as the average length, we find that he has to deal with 2,100 such images during the exhibition. And at any given moment, he must keep 30 images in mind at the same time. Of course, as the number of games gradually tapers off, he has less to think about; but on the other hand, his fatigue begins to tell on him.

So expert are the blindfold geniuses that at the end of every performance they are able to rattle off all the moves of every game, in their exact order with the most astonishing glibness. It sometimes happens during an exhibition that there is a dispute as to the correct position. In such cases, the blindfold player will settle the matter conclusively by calling out all the previous moves; it will be found that he is right, and that his opponent, moving the men on the board, is wrong.

One feature of blindfold play that arouses our curiosity is this: At what rate of speed does the expert play? Does he ponder his moves deeply, averaging say five or six minutes per move? Or—and this is inconceivable, considering his burdens—does he play very rapidly?

Well, suppose we consider a concrete example. The wonderfully gifted British master, Blackburne (page 94), gave a simultaneous exhibition on ten boards only two years after he had learned the moves. He won five games, lost two, and drew three. (This was in 1862, when ten games was the unsurpassed limit for blindfold play.)

Blackburne made 392 moves in his ten games, the session lasting six hours in all. Assuming the master and his opponents played at the same rate of speed, and making no allowance for time consumed in announcing moves, we can make a rough estimate of the time spent per move: 36 seconds per move. So we see that the speed with which the master makes his moves is perhaps the most remarkable feature of his phenomenal skill.

Some masters have specialized in fascinating byways of blindfold chess. Pillsbury, the great American master who lived about the turn of the century (page 101), is considered by some the greatest player who ever lived. He did a great deal to advance the art of blindfold chess, and the feat which particularly delighted his audiences was his playing of twelve games of chess, six games of checkers, and a game of duplicate whist—all at the same time.

An onlooker recalled many years later that "while conducting the card game with all the precision of a fairly good player, he would keep the ever-changing chess and checker positions at his back clearly in his mind's eye, and call off his moves at each board with an accuracy and promptness that looked little short of miraculous. He could break off a seance for an intermission and upon resumption readily call up the positions on every board at will, and, when requested, would announce the moves in any particular game from the beginning."

Pillsbury's most remarkable blindfold performance was his exhibition at Hannover, Germany, in 1902, against 21 minor masters—naturally a far more impressive feat than a contest with 21 carefully selected wooden soldiers. An even more astonishing aspect of this exhibition is that Pillsbury gave it on his bye day in an international tournament, playing his regular tournament games on the day before, and on the day after, the exhibition.

In more recent times, Newell W. Banks, noted American checker master, has played ten games of chess, ten games of checkers, and a game of billiards, all simultaneously. Even more astounding in some ways was the feat of the nineteenth-century organist, Sir Walter Parratt, who made a habit of playing Beethoven sonatas on the organ while conducting two games blindfold.

Authorities and spectators alike are baffled by one feature which is common to all these prodigious feats: the apparent, or relative, absence of strain. This is borne out by the steady rise in the number of games played simultaneously. Incidentally, an achievement which compares with the best that has been produced in this field is Reuben Fine's performance of playing four games blindfold, simultaneously, at the rate of *ten seconds per move.*

How do they do it? So far no one has given a fully satisfactory explanation: geniuses are notoriously better at doing wonderful things than at describing them clearly. There has been no dearth of sensational revelations—Damiano tried that as far back as 1512. The best explanation given so far is that by George Koltanowski in his book *Adventures of a Chess Master.*

Koltanowski cut a chessboard into four sections, and studied the diagonals until he had memorized the color of every square. Once he was thoroughly versed in this, and had an equally firm mastery of the diagonals, he found that he could play over whole scores in his mind without the slightest difficulty. The upshot was that blindfold chess came to him as easily as playing over the board. In a short time he was playing blindfold on twenty boards.

For those who are interested in the psychology of blindfold chess, the following passage from this fascinating book is worth quoting: *

*From Adventures of a Chess Master, by George Koltanowski, edited by Milton Finkelstein. Copyright 1955 by George Koltanowski. Courtesy of David McKay Company, Inc.

"It may be hard to believe, but before I start an exhibition I never know whether I'll be able to remember the positions. However, once started I feel myself possessed of an indescribable power which allows me to think clearly and to play even better chess than I can manage with the board and pieces in sight. Call it will-power if you wish, but when a situation arises which allows me to attempt a combination, I somehow feel that something is possible and manage to see very deeply into the position. Fortunately for me, perhaps, it is at such times that my being blindfolded helps me most of all. My opponents, often thinking that the blindfold player has forgotten the position or will not 'see' their own threats, find weak moves, make them, and are badly beaten. Of course, such thinking on their part is to my advantage, but how many beautiful combinations have never been completed simply because my opponents failed to find the best defense!"

However, we all know that most of us ordinary mortals would make no appreciable progress with such training. Apparently the faculties needed for blindfold play on a large scale are innate. What are they?

It is a matter of common observation that skilful blindfold players have astonishing memories. It is said of Blackburne that when he was shown games in 1899 that he had played in 1862 and had not seen in the intervening 37 years, he readily remembered all the details and effortlessly pointed out mistakes and better lines of play. Pillsbury regularly performed even more remarkable feats of memory. On one occasion two professors gave Pillsbury a grueling memory test. Pillsbury offered to memorize any 30 words read to him once. These were the words selected:

Antiphlogistine, periosteum, takadiastase, plasmon, Threlkeld, streptococcus, staphylococcus, micrococcus, plasmodium, Mississippi, Freiheit, Philadelphia, Cincinnati, athletics, no war, Etchenberg, American, Russian, philosophy, Piet Potgelter's Rost, Salamagundi, Oomisillecootsi, Bangmamvate, Schlechter's Nek, Manyinzama, theosophy, catechism, Madjescomalops. "Pillsbury repeated them in the order given, and then in reverse order, and had no difficulty repeating them the next day!"

The second quality is vivid imagination. Blackburne had an image of every single piece on every single board. A friend said of him that "he thinks in pictures."

The third quality is almost-superhuman concentration. When Blackburne played blindfold chess, he concentrated so profoundly that he lost the senses of touch, taste, and smell.

The fourth quality, and perhaps the most important of all, is "simultaneous alternation." The same friend of Blackburne described this as the power "to remember every detail and then to forget it, to concentrate all one's energy on one point and then shift it like a searchlight to another."

So there are the four necessary qualities for blindfold play. A fifth quality, which is not necessary but generally accompanies them, is a fantastic absent-mindedness in everything else but chess!

RECORD BLINDFOLD PERFORMANCES

PLAYER	NO. OF BOARDS	DATE	PLACE
L. Paulsen	10	1858	Dubuque, Iowa
J. H. Zukertort	16	1876	London
H. N. Pillsbury	22	1902	Moscow
R. Reti	24	1919	Haarlem, Holland
G. Breyer	25	1921	Kaschau, Hungary
A. Alekhine	26	1924	New York
A. Alekhine	28	1925	Paris
R. Reti	29	1925	São Paulo, Brazil
G. Koltanowski	30	1931	Antwerp
A. Alekhine	32	1933	Chicago
G. Koltanowski	34	1937	Edinburgh
M. Najdorf	40	1943	Rosario, Argentine
M. Najdorf	45	1947	São Paulo, Brazil

Among the wealth of beautiful blindfold games the following are noteworthy.

Evans Gambit
Brighton, 1848

	WHITE	BLACK		WHITE	BLACK
	D. Harrwitz	Allies		D. Harrwitz	Allies
1	P—K4	P—K4	7	Castles	P—Q3
2	N—KB3	N—QB3	8	PxP	B—N3
3	B—B4	B—B4	9	N—B3	KN—K2?
4	P—QN4	BxNP	10	N—KN5!	P—Q4
5	P—B3	B—R4	11	NxQP	BxP
6	P—Q4	PxP	12	NxKBP!!	. . . .

If now 12 . . . KxN; 13 NxP dis ch, K—B1; 14 Q—B3ch, B—B3; 15 QxBch!!, PxQ; 16 B—R6 mate. Or 13 . . . K—B3; 14 Q—R5 winning quickly.

12	. . . .	Q—Q2	17	B—B7ch	NxB
13	NxR	BxR	18	QxNch	K—Q1
14	Q—R5ch	P—N3	19	Q—B8ch	Q—K1
15	QxRP	N—Q1	20	R—Q1ch	N—Q4
16	N—B6ch!!	BxN	21	QxBch	Q—K2

White's dynamic attack has bowled over his consulting opponents.

| 22 | RxNch | B—Q2 | 24 | R—K5 | QxR |
| 23 | N—B7ch | K—K1 | 25 | NxQ | Resigns |

Harrwitz played this as one of two blindfold games.

Queen's Fianchetto Defense
Philadelphia, 1859

	WHITE	BLACK		WHITE	BLACK
	P. Morphy	S. Lewis		P. Morphy	S. Lewis
1	P—K4	P—QN3	8	P—B5!	PxP
2	P—Q4	B—N2	9	BxP	B—QB1
3	B—Q3	P—K3	10	BxB	QxB
4	N—KR3!	P—Q4	11	N—B3	P—QB3
5	P—K5	N—K2	12	B—N5	Castles
6	Castles	N—N3	13	BxB	NxB
7	P—KB4!	B—K2	14	Q—R5	P—KR3

White's superior mobility has given him a powerful initiative.

15	R—B3!	N—N3	19	NxN	Q—K2
16	QR—KB1!	Q—K3	20	R—KN3	K—R2
17	N—K2!	N—Q2	21	R/B1—B3!	R—KN1
18	N/K2—B4!	NxN	22	N—R3!	P—N3

White was threatening 23 N—N5ch, K—R1; 24 NxPch, K—R2; 25 Q—N6 mate!

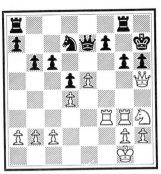

| 23 | N—N5ch! | QxN | 24 | RxPch | K—R1 |

Or 24 . . . R—N2; 25 RxRch, KxR; 26 RxQ and Black cannot reply . . . PxQ.

25   QxQ!   Resigns

For if 25 . . . PxQ; 26 R—R3 mate! Played with three other blindfold games.

Ruy Lopez
Philadelphia, 1897

	WHITE H. N. Pillsbury	BLACK S. W. Bampton		WHITE H. N. Pillsbury	BLACK S. W. Bampton
1	P—K4	P—K4	8	N—K5	Castles
2	N—KB3	N—QB3	9	N—QB3	B—B3
3	B—N5	N—B3	10	B—B4	R—K1
4	Castles	NxP	11	N—N4	BxP
5	P—Q4	N—Q3	12	N—Q5	B—K4
6	B—R4	P—K5	13	NxB	NxN
7	R—K1	B—K2	14	Q—R5	P—KB3

Pillsbury has sacrificed two Pawns for a promising attack.

15	B—QN3	K—R1	17	Q—R4	R—K3
16	R—K3	P—KN3	18	R—KR3	P—KR4

Having provoked weaknesses in Black's King side, White is now ready for further sacrifices.

19	NxKBP	N—B4	22	RxPch	N/B2—R3
20	Q—N5	N—B2	23	QxQch	RxQ
21	QxNP	QxN	24	B—K5	K—N2

Having simplified forcefully, Pillsbury now wins at least a Rook.

25	P—KN4!	NxP	31	K—R1	R—KB1
26	R—N5ch	K—R3	32	R—N1ch	N—N5
27	BxR	NxB	33	RxKP	K—B4
28	RxN	K—N3	34	R—K2	R—K1
29	R—K5	P—Q3	35	R/N1—K1!	N—K4
30	R—K7	B—R6	36	P—KB4!	KxP

Now Pillsbury winds up the game very neatly.

37	R—B2ch	K—N4	40	B—B3	R—K6
38	B—Q5	P—B3	41	BxN	BxB
39	R—N1ch	N—N5	42	R/B2—N2	Resigns

A marvelous effort against a player of near-master strength in a blindfold exhibition on 20 boards.

Bishop's Opening
Odessa, 1918

| | WHITE | BLACK | | WHITE | BLACK |
	B. Gons-siorovsky	A. Alekhine		B. Gons-siorovsky	A. Alekhine
1	P—K4	P—K4	7	BxP	Castles
2	B—B4	N—KB3	8	N—Q2	PxP
3	P—Q3	P—B3	9	B—QN3	P—QR4!
4	Q—K2	B—K2	10	P—B3?	P—R5
5	P—B4	P—Q4!	11	B—B2	P—R6!
6	KPxP	KPxP	12	P—QN3	R—K1!

Playing with his usual verve, Alekhine has seized the initiative.

13	Castles	B—QN5!	16	KN—B3	P—Q5!
14	Q—B2	BxP	17	KR—K1	B—N7ch
15	B—N5	N—B3	18	K—N1	N—Q4!!

Threatening . . . N—B6 mate.

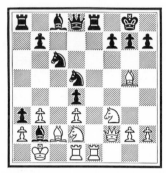

19	RxRch	QxR	22	R—K1?!	B—B4!
20	N—K4	QxN!!	23	RxQ	PxR
21	B—Q2	Q—K6!!	24	Q—B1	. . . .

Alekhine now announced mate in three by 24 . . . PxB; 25 B—Q1, N/B3—N5! and 26 . . . N—B6 mate. (One of six blindfold games.)

Max Lange Attack
Antwerp, 1929

	WHITE G. Kolta- nowski	BLACK P. Dunkel- blum		WHITE G. Kolta- nowski	BLACK P. Dunkel- blum
1	P—K4	P—K4	8	R—K1ch	B—K3
2	N—KB3	N—QB3	9	N—N5	Q—Q4
3	B—B4	B—B4	10	N—QB3	Q—B4
4	Castles	N—B3	11	QN—K4	B—QN5
5	P—Q4	PxP	12	P—QB3	PxP
6	P—K5	P—Q4	13	PxP	B—R4?
7	PxN	PxB	14	P—N4!	Q—N3

The disorganized state of Black's game presents White with good attacking chances.

15	NxB	PxN	19	Q—K1!	R—KB1
16	P—B7ch	KxP?	20	R—K8!	Q—Q2
17	N—N5ch	K—N1	21	RxRch	KxR
18	RxP	Q—Q6	22	B—R3ch	N—K2

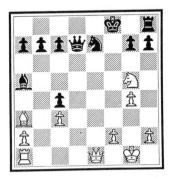

The pin on Black's Knight proves his undoing as White relentlessly drives off the Black Queen. The finish is very pretty.

23	R—Q1!	QxPch	24	K—B1!!	QxN
			25	R—Q5!!	. . . .

Because of White's last move, the Rook cannot be captured with check. If 25 . . . QxR White mates in two moves.

25	. . . .	Q—R5	26	R—R5!!	Q—B3
			27	R—KB5!	Resigns

A wonderful example of the power of the pin. This was one of ten blindfold games.

Postal Chess

Postal chess, also known as "correspondence chess" and "chess by mail," has been played for many years. Up to recent times, however, its enthusiasts were mostly shut-ins or players who lived in towns that lacked chess clubs. About 1940 postal chess experienced an enormous increase in popularity, which shows no signs of abating.

Many chessplayers have discovered the attractions of postal play in recent years. Since consulting books is permissible, the postal player is able to school himself in the openings and perfect his theoretical knowledge. The more generous time limit is appreciated by players who find it hard to accommodate themselves to the requirements of the rigorous time limit for over-the-board play.

Postal play is particularly helpful to young players who are eager to improve their game. The postal player has adequate time to work out the details of a complicated middle-game maneuver or a tricky endgame rich in finesse. And, of course, those who are shy or self-conscious about their play are able to complete their games in the privacy of den or study. Other players whose long business hours or travels keep them from a chess club, as well as those who have moved to the suburbs, are among the others who benefit from postal chess.

While postal chess is very enjoyable, it has its own special problems that require special attention. Following is a list of rules for postal play evolved by *Chess Review* for its tournaments. Not all these rules are applicable to postal play in general; however, familiarity with the rules will give useful sidelights on the problems which are uniquely associated with postal play.

Anyone who wishes to play postal chess must bear in mind that mastery of the chess notation is indispensable for this type of play.

1. The Laws of Chess (Official Code of the International Federation of Chess) governs all games, except as herein modified or as obviously inapplicable to Postal Chess.

2. Players must use standard "Descriptive Notation" in sending moves. The symbol "N" should be used to represent the Knight. A full, clear, and correct return address and tournament section number must accompany each move.

3. Each move must be accompanied by the following dates: (1) the date of receipt of the opponent's previous move; (2) the date by which the sender expects his move to be postmarked, judging by the time at which he will post it and the time of mail collections.

4. In sending moves, players must correctly acknowledge the opponent's previous moves and designate the correct number of each move. Acknowledgment must cover the move immediately previous and any others not already acknowledged; e.g., any accepted series of "if" moves (cf. Rule 9), also diagram (cf. Rule 6). Failure correctly to acknowledge a move should be immediately challenged (cf. also Rule 5).

5. A player who has dispatched a move must abide by the record that he has mailed. He may not alter it, by addition or otherwise, except as under Rules 6 and 7. If he sends two or more moves for the same turn to play, the earliest (as judged by postmarks) must stand as made. If a player disputes his opponent's acknowledgment of a move, he must ask it to be corrected before play may continue or that the original record (postcard) of his move be submitted to the Postal Chess Editor for verification.

6. If a player sends an ambiguous move capable of more than

one legal interpretation, his opponent should ask which interpreta-tion is meant, before sending his reply-move. A check identifies a move which would otherwise be ambiguous (e.g., B—N5ch is sufficient; so B—KN5ch or B—QN5ch is not necessary). But omission of the announcement of a check is *not* sufficient (B—KN5 is necessary even if B—QN5 would be with a check).

If the opponent replies without mentioning the ambiguity, the player should specify which of the legal moves, consistent with the record, he had intended; and the game must revert to the specified move. Any different interpretation which may have been adopted and the move made in reply to such are thereupon an-nulled.

If a player submits a clear diagram of his position with a move, it shall be a part of the record of that move. Hence any error of recording thus revealed should be reported and corrected as for an ambiguity occurring on that move.

7. If a player sends an illegal or "impossible" move, the opponent should note it as such and call for a legal move. The illegal move may be replaced by any legal move. In Postal Chess, a false check or absence of announcement of a check renders a move illegal. Moves erased or otherwise visibly altered must be dealt with *at once* as illegal moves.

8. Any player who repeatedly sends faultily recorded moves (cf. Rules 2–7) should be reported to and warned by the Postal Chess Editor. Thereafter, forfeit may follow, at the discretion of the Postal Chess Editor, for further delay of this sort.

9. If a player assumes that his opponent will make certain moves and sends hypothetic replies ("if" moves), they shall not be binding unless the opponent makes the moves assumed. If he does, the game must follow the suggested continuation (or any accepted part of it) exactly as written, provided the moves are legal. For such extra moves, the opponent may take extra time: 24 hours maximum per 2 "if" moves; plus 24 hours for any odd "if" moves.

10. If a player abandons his games in any section, or with-

draws, all his unfinished games in the tourney will be defaulted and scored as full points for his opponents. Withdrawing players should notify their opponents and the Postal Chess Editor.

If a player withdraws within eight weeks after play has started, or without sending more than 6 moves, a new player shall be substituted in his place.

11. At the end of each game, the winner (or White in the case of a draw) shall report the result to the Postal Chess Editor. He must report within 72 hours. The opponent may also report to ensure prompt recording; but he *must* then specify that his report is *by the loser* (or *by Black,* if the game was drawn).

12. The following time regulations must be strictly observed: a player has 72 hours maximum (but cf. Rule 9) in which to reply from receipt of each move. Sundays, legal holidays, and the time a move is in transit are not counted. Each player may also take "time out" for up to four weeks (consecutively or a week at a time) per year, *provided* he notifies each opponent and the Postal Chess Editor *in advance.*

13. A player may claim a win by forfeit if his opponent oversteps the time limit; but for such claim to be considered it must be accompanied by the following:

   (a) Opponent's name and address, and the number of the tournament section;

   (b) The game score up to the last move made;

   (c) The original records (postcards) of the last 2 moves received (plus "repeats");

   (d) A list of these dates: when claimant mailed his latest move, any "repeat" of it, and his claim, and dates of receipt of opponent's last 2 moves;

   (e) A statement of the time normally taken by the mail in transit.

On receipt of such claim the Postal Chess Editor shall request parallel information of the opponent. If the opponent does not send this within two weeks, the claim shall be allowed, conditional on subsequent proof that reply was impossible (e.g., because of illness). If the reply is made and comparison of statements and/or postmarks shows the opponent violated the time limit, the claim will be allowed (but see below).

The Postal Chess Editor may exercise discretion on forfeitures. For first offenders, he issues only a warning (but shall record the fact and date of warning for future reference). If the statements of claimant and opponent do not agree as to dates or other facts, he will be governed by consideration of their previous records and, at need, may request statements of the experience of other players in the tourney. For a player with a reasonably clear record, illness or business emergency may be allowed as a valid reason for delay of reasonable duration. *Note also* that no claim for forfeit shall be honored if the claimant's last 2 moves prove to have been sent without a proper return address or proper dates as in Rules 2 and 3.

14. A player may cite an opponent for lateness, without claim for forfeit, by simply reporting the fact with opponent's name, address, and tournament section number. The Postal Chess Editor shall then attempt to get the game resumed but shall not record the incident for future reference or punitive action except at his own discretion.

15. Delays should not be neglected; and the Postal Chess Editor may rule a double forfeit if both players let their game be unreasonably delayed.

16. Any player who writes in a discourteous or offensive manner to an opponent shall be warned by the Postal Chess Editor and may be barred from further tournament play and all his games forfeited for any such offense thereafter.

17. All disputes and disagreements shall be referred to the Postal Chess Editor and the decision rendered shall be final.

Playing at Odds

Though odds-giving is no longer as popular as it once was, it still remains the only way in which a weak player can put up a fight against a much stronger player. Odds-giving consists in one player's removing one or more of his forces from the board before the beginning of the game. The usual forms of odds are:

Odds of the Queen

Odds of the Queen Rook

Odds of the Queen Knight

Odds of the King Bishop Pawn and move (or two moves)

There are also certain forms of odds that have now become obsolete. These include the odds of the "capped Pawn," by which a player undertook to checkmate with a specific Pawn.

Of Queen odds there is little to say, because this piece is so valuable that such odds can only be given where the difference in playing strength is enormous. Even a slight improvement in the game of the weaker player will make it impossible to give him the odds.

Here is a good example of a game at Queen odds:

Remove White's Queen
Nuremberg, 1890

	WHITE *Dr. S. Tarrasch*	BLACK *C. Schroeder*		WHITE *Dr. S. Tarrasch*	BLACK *C. Schroeder*
1	P—K4	P—K4	3	P—Q3	P—KB4
2	P—KB4	P—Q3	4	N—QB3	BPxP

147

5	QPxP	P—QR3	9	R—Q1	Q—KN3??
6	PxP	PxP	10	R—Q8ch	K—B2
7	N—B3	B—QN5	11	B—B4ch	any
8	B—KN5	Q—Q3?	12	NxP mate	

This is a typical odds game: Black lost by opening up the position for his opponent's pieces; by losing time; and by failing to give up his Queen (move 9) to stop checkmate.

Games with the odds of Queen Rook are more of a struggle; the implication is, after all, that the odds-receiver is too strong to be given a Queen.

There are a number of rules of thumb for the odds-receiver to observe, for example:

1. Don't let your opponent play a gambit, in which he can baffle you with his superior combinative skill. (Play 1 . . . P—K3 or 1 . . . P—QB4 in answer to his 1 P—K4.)

2. Play out your pieces rapidly, especially those that make it possible for you to castle early. This will save your King from early exposure to attack.

3. Avoid moving pieces or Pawns more than once; avoid playing Knights to the Rook 3 square, where they will be out of play.

4. Be sure to move the King Pawn and Queen Pawn, in order to open up developing lines for your Bishops; but be wary of moving the other Pawns, except possibly the Queen Bishop Pawn and the King Bishop Pawn.

5. Once you have developed your minor pieces, it is time to play out your Queen and move the Queen Rook to a center file or one near the center. (For example: . . . Q—Q2, or . . . Q—K2, followed by . . . QR—K1 or . . . QR—Q1.)

In the middle game these rules will prove useful:

1. At each move, watch for possible captures, sacrifices, checks,

or threats for these are the moves by which a game is decided.

2. If you have the initiative and see a chance for a promising sacrifice, don't hesitate to make it, especially if you can get several Pawns in return. Remember that you are starting out with an initial material advantage, and that you can afford to part with some material.

3. Keep exchanging pieces. The more pieces you remove in this way, the more valuable your material advantage becomes and the less chance there is that you will lose out in the mid-game complications. Above all, offer exchanges of the Queens. Such offers of exchanges gain time whenever your opponent has to retreat in order to evade the exchange.

Here is a game in which Black violates many of the foregoing rules and speedily comes a cropper:

Remove White's Queen Rook
Two Knights' Defense
New Orleans, 1858

	WHITE	BLACK		WHITE	BLACK
	P. Morphy	*Amateur*		*P. Morphy*	*Amateur*
1	P—K4	P—K4	7	Q—B3ch	K—K3
2	N—KB3	N—QB3	8	N—B3	N—Q5?
3	B—B4	N—B3	9	BxNch	K—Q3
4	N—N5	P—Q4	10	Q—B7	B—K3?
5	PxP	NxP	11	BxB	NxB
6	NxBP?!	KxN	12	N—K4ch	K—Q4

Black's inexact play has exposed his King as a target.

13	P—QB4ch!	KxN	16	Q—K2ch	K—B7
14	QxN	Q—Q5?	17	P—Q3ch!	KxB
15	Q—N4ch	K—Q6	18	Castles mate!	

A delightful conclusion—and a frightening warning at the same time!

In the following game Black is daring enough to accept a gambit, but his play is very dashing and knowing.

Remove White's Queen Rook
Bishop's Gambit
New Orleans, 1855

WHITE	BLACK		WHITE	BLACK
P. Morphy	*C. A. Maurian*		*P. Morphy*	*C. A. Maurian*
1 P—K4	P—K4	6	N—KB3	Q—R4
2 P—KB4	PxP	7	P—Q4	N—B3
3 B—B4	Q—R5ch	8	B—N3	B—R3
4 K—B1	P—QN4	9	Q—K2	NxQP!!
5 B—Q5	N—QB3	10	NxN	P—N5!!

Very unusual play from an odds-receiver!

| 11 | QxB | Q—Q8ch | 12 | K—B2 | N—N5 mate |

At the somewhat smaller odds of Queen Knight, Black's play must be correspondingly more careful. Here are some pointers for the opening:

1. Get your pieces out quickly and avoid gambits that are likely to get your King into trouble. Note in the first game at these odds, for example, how rapidly White's Queen Rook swings into action due to the absence of White's Queen Knight.

2. Play defenses where the absence of the Queen Knight is noticeable. For instance, after 1 P—K4, P—Q4; 2 PxP, QxP, White is unable to drive Black's Queen away with 3 N—QB3. The Center Counter, Falkbeer Counter, and Sicilian and French Defense are all good lines for Black at these odds.

3. Playing very close, blockaded defenses has the virtue of setting up a fairly safe position. However, this favors the stronger player too. Thus, exchanges are avoided so that he can hold on to his attacking pieces. Then too, the odds-giver often finds ingenious ways to break through (as in the Tarrasch game below). Such breakthroughs are often aided by the odds-receiver's blissful unawareness of what his crafty opponent has in store for him.

4. As a rule, the odds-receiver does best with straightforward development plus relentless insistence on exchanges.

Remove White's Queen Knight
Muzio Gambit
London, 1865

WHITE	BLACK		WHITE	BLACK
W. Steinitz	*Van der Meden*		*W. Steinitz*	*Van der Meden*
1 P—K4	P—K4	7	P—K5!	QxP
2 P—KB4	PxP	8	BxPch!?	KxB
3 N—KB3	P—KN4	9	P—Q4!	QxPch
4 B—B4	P—N5	10	B—K3	Q—B3
5 Castles	PxN	11	Q—R5ch	Q—N3
6 QxP	Q—B3	12	RxPch	N—B3

13	RxNch!	KxR	17	Q—Q5ch!	Q—K3
14	B—Q4ch	K—B2	18	Q—KN5!	Q—KR3
15	R—B1ch!	K—N1	19	Q—Q8ch	B—B1
16	Q—K5!	B—N2	20	Q—K8!!	Resigns

Remove White's Queen Knight
Center Counter Game
Nuremberg, 1890

WHITE	BLACK		WHITE	BLACK
Dr. S. Tar-rasch	K. Meiser		Dr. S. Tar-rasch	K. Meiser
1 P—K4	P—Q4!	8	QxB	N—R3
2 P—K5	P—Q5?	9	Q—R3	Q—Q2
3 P—KB4	P—QB4	10	Q—QN3	N—R4
4 B—B4	N—QB3	11	P—K6!	Q—B3
5 N—B3	B—N5?	12	Q—KR3	R—Q1?
6 BxPch!	KxB	13	Castles	P—KN3
7 N—N5ch	K—K1	14	P—B5!	. . . .

Profiting by his opponent's slips, White has built up a powerful game. If now 14 . . . NxP??; 15 RxN!, PxR; 16 Q—R5 mate.

14	. . . .	B—N2	19	B—Q2	P—N3
15	PxP	R—Q4	20	Q—N3!	N—N2
16	N—B7!	NxN	21	QR—K1	N—Q1
17	NPxNch	K—B1	22	R—K4!	R—Q3
18	P—Q3	P—KR3	23	R—N4!	NxKP

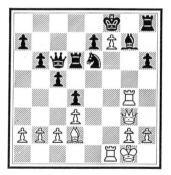

24	RxB!!	NxR	27	P—B8/Qch	K—N3
25	BxP!!	KRxB	28	Q—B7ch	K—N4
26	QxNch!!	KxQ	29	Q—B5ch	K—R5
			30	P—N3 mate	

White's charming combination brilliantly exploited Black's lapses.

Remove White's Queen Knight
Center Counter Game
London, 1859

	WHITE *P. Morphy*	BLACK *E. Pindar*		WHITE *P. Morphy*	BLACK *E. Pindar*
1	P—K4	P—Q4!	11	Castles (K)	R—K1
2	PxP	QxP	12	QR—K1	Q—Q3
3	P—QB4	Q—Q1	13	P—B4	P—B4
4	P—Q4	P—K4!	14	BPxP	RxP
5	B—Q3	B—N5ch!	15	RxR	QxR
6	B—Q2	BxBch	16	R—K1	Q—Q3
7	QxB	N—QB3!	17	Q—N5	B—Q2
8	N—K2	N—B3	18	R—KB1	R—K1
9	P—Q5	N—Q5!	19	P—N4	P—QN3
10	N—N3	Castles	20	Q—R4	P—KR3

Even the great Morphy is helpless against the admirable solidity of Black's play.

21	PxP	PxP	24	Q—Q8ch	Q—B1
22	P—KR3	R—K6	25	QxB	RxB
23	N—K4	NxN	26	R—K1	N—KB3
			27	Q—B7	N—B4 and wins

The odds of Pawn and move, or Pawn and two moves, lead to subtle play that taxes the abilities of both players. On the one hand, Black's King is exposed to danger and may readily succumb to a brisk attack; in addition, Black's game is generally cramped. On the other hand, the material odds are really slight, and Black's open King Bishop file will often yield him the initiative.

Remove Black's King Bishop Pawn
Match, 1865

	WHITE C. de Vere	BLACK W. Steinitz		WHITE C. de Vere	BLACK W. Steinitz
1	P—K4	P—Q3	11	P—B4	P—Q4
2	P—Q4	N—KB3	12	P—QN3	P—B4
3	N—QB3	P—K3	13	KPxP	KPxP
4	N—B3	N—B3	14	Q—K3!	QPxP
5	B—QN5	P—QR3	15	N—B5	R—B2
6	BxNch	PxB	16	R—K1	N—Q4
7	Castles	B—K2	17	Q—K6	B—B3
8	Q—Q3	Castles	18	N—K5!	BxN
9	N—K2	P—QR4	19	RxB	N—N5
10	N—N3	B—R3	20	N—R6ch!	. . . .

20	. . . .	PxN	21	BxP	Q—B3
			22	R—N5ch	QxR

Or 22 . . . K—R1; 23 QxQch, RxQ; 24 B—N7ch etc.

23   BxQ and wins

Remove Black's King Bishop Pawn
Nuremberg, 1888

WHITE	BLACK		WHITE	BLACK
K. Eckart	*Dr. S. Tarrasch*		*K. Eckart*	*Dr. S. Tarrasch*
1 P—K4	N—QB3	9	B—N5ch	P—B3!
2 P—KB4	P—K4	10	PxP	Castles!
3 N—KB3	PxP	11	PxPch	KxP
4 B—B4	B—B4	12	B—B6ch	K—N3
5 P—Q4	NxP?!	13	Q—Q3	RxN!
6 NxN	Q—R5ch	14	Q—N5ch	K—B2
7 K—B1	P—Q4	15	Q—N7ch	K—Q3
8 PxP	B—KN5	16	N—B3	. . . .

16	. . . .	Q—B7ch!!	17	KxQ	R—Q8 dis ch
			18	B—K3	BxB mate

Odds-giving can also form the basis of a "handicap" tournament, in which each player is graded according to the odds he receives. Thus, if A gives Rook odds to B and C, then B and C play each other even. If A gives D Knight odds, then D gives B and C odds of Pawn and move. If A gives E Pawn and move, then E gives B and C Knight odds, and gives D odds of Pawn and move. Similarly all the other players are graded according to the odds relationship that prevails.

After the tournament is over, the odds can be modified according to the odds. The famous City of London Chess Club had an annual handicap tournament for many years, but such a contest has become rather old fashioned in recent years.

Chess Problems

By P. L. Rothenberg

A chess problem is a composed position with a specified stipulation, the fulfilment of which is the required solution. Almost invariably, the stipulation in chess problems calls for a solution in a *specified* number of moves.

In the orthodox chess problem, the most commonly known, White, moving first, must deliver mate in a specified number of moves, against Black's best defense. The fact that White, as a rule, has an overwhelming force and can easily "win" is immaterial—for the one and only object is to mate the Black King in *no more* than the stipulated number of moves. The rules of the game of chess govern the play involved in solving a problem. The orthodox chess problems (also known as "direct-mate" problems) mostly in vogue at present are two-movers and three-movers. Longer-range settings are uncommon.

When the terms "problem" or "chess problem" are used henceforth, it is to be understood that reference is made to the orthodox direct-mate problem.

A chess problem is distinguishable from a *natural endgame* (one arising in a game of chess, in which a draw or a win for either side is to be conclusively demonstrated) or a *composed ending* (one in which the composer's stipulation calls for the conclusive demonstration of a draw or a win for a given side).

This is not intended as an exhaustive study of chess problems; it is rather an introduction to the reader of a phase of chess on which there is a vast literature, the earliest records dating back to the ninth century—over 1,100 years ago! (See Bibliography, page 188.)

In the course of centuries (and more so during the past fifty to one hundred years), the composers of chess problems have evolved rules and standards which have governed the art of composition. In the absence of compelling considerations which inherently disallow faithful compliance with standard practices, the following criteria are universally accepted as sound guides for the composition of chess problems:

1. *Legality.* A chess problem position must be one which could have *conceivably* arisen in an ordinary game of chess, however unlikely the setting may be. This requisite is a *must.* A setting which, say, contains more Pawn captures by one side than the number of missing pieces in the force of the other side is impossible—hence, it is illegal and unsound.

2. *Economy of Force.* The aim always is to create the desired idea with a minimum of force. This, of course, is not a mere quantitative consideration, for it must be recognized that the expression of some themes requires the use of a substantial force. Consequently, it does not follow that the more slender of two positions is necessarily the superior one. It is, however, fundamental that *every* piece in a problem position *must* perform a specific function, and no piece must be included unless its presence is absolutely necessary. Also, use of promoted pieces in the set position of a problem is rarely, if ever, condoned.

3. *Richness of Theme and Variations.* A chess problem without a theme, or without some striking idea at the very least, is, as a rule, without merit, however intricate and complicated the mating nets may be. The theme, in effect, corresponds to the plot of a literary composition, and it should be expressed in a rich, clear, convincing manner. The richer a problem is in thematic and otherwise significant variations, the better it is rated. As a matter of fact, rare is the single-line problem which merits recognition.

4. *One Solution.* A chess problem must have one solution only— the one intended by the composer. Problems yielding to more than one *intended* solutions are a rarity, and are sometimes composed as a novelty, a joke, or a trap to plague participants in a problem-solving tournament. Ordinarily, therefore, a problem having more than one solution is unsound.

5. Duals. A "dual" is a *choice* of moves available to White in response to a move by Black. When this occurs in the thematic variation of a problem, the setting, as a rule, is considered to be unsound. Minor duals are not regarded as serious defects, except that some composers measure the merit of a problem by the complete absence of duals of any sort.

6. Key Move. The key move, to meet the most acceptable artistic standards, should be a "quiet" one—that is, it should not be a check; it should not be the capture of a man; it should not restrict the freedom of the Black King (or that of any other unit in the Black force, unless the very theme calls for it). Generally, key moves in first-rate problems easily meet the stated requisites. Moreover, the key move should never be an obvious maneuver. A surprise key move, that is, one that is least expected, is a splendid feature. A thematic key move, that is, one leading to expression of the theme which but for the key move could not be expressed, is an artistic feature which is a *must* in the composition of many problems.

7. Miscellaneous. There are numerous additional refinements in the composition of chess problems which are not within the scope of our discussion. It may be added that a basic feature is originality—the creation of a new theme or the novel presentation of an existing one. Another significant feature is the existence of good tries, that is, attempted key moves which are thwarted by subtle Black defenses.

In gaining some conception of the standards governing composition, the reader should be in a position to look for certain features which will enable him the better to understand a chess problem and the more intelligently to solve it. Moreover, it will be found profitable to try to account for the presence of each individual piece in a problem setting.

TERMS

Basically, chess-problem terminology is the same as that used in the game of chess, and just as prevalent are terms such as *rank*, *file, diagonal, threat, defense, sacrifice, interference, variation*, etc., etc. A great many terms, however, have inevitably arisen as nomenclatures for the various elements of chess problems which have been evolved and developed in the course of years. These, essentially, account for a somewhat specialized vocabulary.

An alphabetical listing of the more commonly known chess problem terms is given below. This is followed by an alphabetical listing of the better-known chess-problem themes, with illustrative diagrams of chess problems appended.

A.C.W. SERIES *See* **Christmas Series.**

AFTER Inserted between the names of two composers, the word *after* indicates that the first name has revised a composition previously created by the other. *See* Problem No. 4, "by P. L. Rothenberg *after* Alain White" (page 173).

ANTICIPATION Prior creation of a problem or an identical idea in a problem. To say that a problem by Jones has been *anticipated* is to indicate that a composer other than Jones has already composed it in identical or substantially similar form.

BATTERY The line-up of two pieces of the same color on a rank, file, or diagonal, so that when the interfering piece is removed from the line, the remaining piece controls the line. The removal of the piece from the line is called "firing" of the *battery*.

Direct Battery When removal of the interfering piece from the line results in a discovered check or discovered checkmate of the enemy King by the remaining piece. *See* Problem No. 11 (page 180). The White Rook on KB6 and White Bishop on KN7 constitute a *direct battery*.

Indirect Battery When removal of the interfering piece from the line results in control by the remaining piece of a square (or squares) other than that occupied by the enemy King, but usually in the enemy King's field. *See* Problem No. 8. The White Rook on KN6 and the White Bishop on KR7 constitute an *indirect battery*.

Masked Battery When an enemy piece is also in the line-up and it has to be removed from the line before the battery can be fired. *See* Problem No. 12. If a Black Knight, say, were stationed on Black's KN6, we would have a *masked battery*.

BLOCK *See* **Block Position.**

BLOCK POSITION A problem setting wherein White has a ready mate for *every* possible Black move. *See* Problem No. 1. (Note particularly that in chess-problem terminology the term *block* is distinguishable from the meaning of the word in the usual sense—that of blocking a piece by another of the same color.)

Incomplete Block Position A problem setting wherein White has a ready mate for all but one or several possible moves by Black. *See* Problem No. 7, where White has no ready mates for 1 . . . B—KN2, 1 . . . B—R3, 1 . . . P—R4, 1 . . . R—K2, and 1 . . . R—Q3, but does have a ready mate for all other Black moves.

BLOCK THREAT A *block position* in which the key move executes a threat, and in that respect differs from the key moves in *Simile Waiters, Added-Mate Waiters,* and *Mutates,* which are covered under "themes," beginning on page 170.

CHAMELEON ECHO *See* **Echo.**

CHECK

Cross-Check A check (or checkmate) by one side in response to a check by the other, but *not* by means of capturing the checking enemy piece. *See* variation in Problem No. 12: 1 . . . PxNch; 2 R—QR4 mate.

Discovered Check The firing of a *direct battery* resulting in delivery of check to the enemy King. For example, any move by the White Bishop at QN5, in Problem No. 11, results in a *discovered check.*

CHRISTMAS PROBLEMS Chess-problem positions of a humorous, fantastic, or generally unorthodox nature, composed, as a rule, as Christmas and New Year holiday greetings.

CHRISTMAS SERIES A collection of over 40 books on chess problems, sponsored (1905–1936) by the greatest authority on chess problems of all time, the late Alain White, an American (1880–1951). Most of the books in the series were authored or edited by Alain White, either solely or in collaboration with other eminent authorities. The collection derives its name from a a curious sidelight. As new volumes appeared, White sent them as Christmas gifts to chess-problem enthusiasts the world over. The collection is also known as the A.C.W. Series. Mr. White, however, dropped his middle initial during the latter years of his life.

CONDITIONAL PROBLEMS   Chess problems in which the stipulated conditions—such as, e.g., that mate *must* be delivered with a specified piece—do not follow the standard rules of the game of chess. These problems were popular in the nineteenth century.

CONSTRUCTION PROBLEMS   Settings in which the task consists of an arrangement of pieces for the purpose of illustrating a·striking feature, such as, e.g., a legal position in which a *maximum* number of mates can be delivered on the move by either side or by both; or a legal array of all 32 pieces, with one side stalemated and the other having *minimum* mobility, and the like.

CONTINGENT THREAT   A secondary threat which arises when Black attempts to meet the primary threat exerted by White.

COOK   A solution in addition to and other than that intended by the composer; also used as a verb.

CRITICAL MOVE   *See Indian* theme, page 176.

CROSS-CHECK   *See* **Check.**

DECALET   A problem setting containing a total of exactly 10 pieces. This term was coined by the editors of *Chess Review,* leading American magazine on the game of chess, when it conducted a problem-composing tournament (1942–43) in commemorating the tenth anniversary of its founding.

DECOY   Luring an enemy piece into a less favorable position. *See Roman* theme (page 185) and Problem No. 15.

DIRECT BATTERY   *See* **Battery.**

DIRECT-MATE PROBLEM   The orthodox chess problem in which it is stipulated that White, moving first, is to deliver mate in a specified number of moves. *See* Problems Nos. 1–17.

DISCOVERED CHECK   *See* **Check.**

DISCOVERED MATE   *See* **Mate.**

DUAL   A choice of moves available to White in response to a move by Black. *See* Problem No. 10. Were Black aimlessly to respond to White's key move with 1 . . . P—R6, for example, *dual* continuations would be available to White, as shown in the solution of the problem.

DUAL MATE A choice of mating moves available to White. *See* Problem No. 7. After 1 . . . B—KN2, White is able to mate by 2 QxP or 2 Q—N6.

ECHO; CHAMELEON ECHO Repeated occurrence, in a *different* part of the chessboard, of a position, in identical or substantially identical form, especially in connection with the mate delivered by White. When the Black King in the duplicated position is on a square of opposite color from that in the sister setting, we have a *Chameleon Echo*. *See* Problem No. 4. The *echo* is shown in the variations following 1 . . . R—Q1 and 1 . . . Castles.

ECHO MATE *See* **Echo; Mate.**

ECONOMICAL MATE *See* **Mate.**

FAIRY PROBLEMS Chess problems of an unorthodox nature in which the stipulations, conditions, or actual pieces used are deliberate deviations from the basic rules and regulations of the game of chess. *See* **Christmas Problems; Helpmate Problems.**

FIRING OF THE BATTERY *See* **Battery.**

FLIGHT or FLIGHT SQUARE A square to which the Black King has access. See Problem No. 12, in which the Black King has two flight squares—K4 and B2. *See* **King's Field.**

Flight Capture Occurs when the Black King's flight consists of capture of a White piece.

Star Flight Access of the Black King to each of the four diagonally adjacent squares. If the K2 and B4 squares were also available to the Black King in Problem No. 12—in addition to K4 and B2, which are already available—the King would have a *star flight*.

FORSYTH NOTATION A system of recording positions, as follows:

1. All squares are accounted for, rank by rank, from left to right, beginning with White's 8th rank and ending with White's 1st rank.

2. The White pieces are designated by upper-case letters; the Black pieces by lower-case letters; the blank squares by actual numerical count.

For example, the position of Problem No. 16: klN5;P2p4; 4p3;2p5;7b;8;8;6QK.

GIVE & TAKE KEY or **GIVE & TAKE KEY MOVE** A *key move* which deprives the Black King of existing *flight squares,* but which creates *at least* as many new ones. *See* **Key Move; Restrictive Key.**

HALF-PIN Occurs when two Black pieces are stationed on the same line between the White Queen or White Rook or White Bishop and the Black King, so that if one of the two Black pieces is removed from the line, the remaining one is pinned. *See* Problem No. 9. If a Black piece were stationed on Black's QB3 or Q4, we would have a *half-pin.*

HELPMATE or **HELPMATE PROBLEMS** A *Fairy* chess problem in which one side deliberately co-operates with the other in enabling it to deliver mate in a specified number of moves. In *helpmates,* as a rule, Black moves first and helps White deliver mate.

IDEA *See* **Theme.**

ILLEGAL POSITION *See* **Legal Position.**

IMPOSSIBLE POSITION *See* **Legal Position.**

INCOMPLETE BLOCK or **INCOMPLETE BLOCK POSITION** *See* **Block Position.**

INDIRECT BATTERY *See* **Battery.**

IRREAL POSITION *See* **Legal Position.**

KEY *See* **Key Move.**

KEY MOVE The very first move made by White leading to solution of the chess problem. *See* **Give & Take Key; Restrictive Key.**

KEY PIECE The White piece which makes the *key move.*

KING'S FIELD The squares contiguous to the square on which the King stands. The *King's field* consists of a maximum of 8 squares, when the King is *not* on the edge of the chessboard;

or a minimum of 3 squares, when the King is in the corner.

LEGALITY *See* **Legal Position.**

LEGAL MOVE One that is permitted in accordance with the rules of the game of chess. Determining the legality of moves frequently arises in **Retrograde Analysis** (*which see*).

LEGAL POSITION One that can conceivably arise in an ordinary game of chess, subject to complete compliance with the rules of the game. If a position fails to meet this requisite, it is termed *illegal, impossible,* or *irreal.*

LETTER PROBLEM A chess problem setting in the physical form of a letter of the alphabet.

LINE Rank, file, or diagonal.

LONG-RANGE PROBLEM An orthodox chess problem the solution of which is stipulated in *more* than 3 moves. There is no universal agreement, however, on this point, for there is conflict of authority on what constitutes a clear-cut line of division between the normal and the long-range setting.

LOYDESQUE Characterizing unique originality, surprise, brilliance, or unusual flight of fancy in chess problems. After the great American chess-problem composer and creator of puzzles, Sam Loyd (1841–1911). *See* Problem Nos. 2, 7, 11 & 13—No. 11 especially.

MAJOR DUAL *See* **Thematic Dual.**

MAN Queen, Rook, Bishop, or Knight—as distinguishable from King or Pawn.

MASKED BATTERY *See* **Battery.**

MATE

> *Discovered Mate* The firing of a *direct battery* resulting in delivery of mate. *See* mates following all moves by White Rook in Problem No. 12.

> *Echo Mate* Repeated occurrence, in a *different* part of the chessboard, of a mating position, in identical or substantially identical form, such as the mates following 1 . . . R—Q1 and 1 . . . Castles, in Problem No. 4. *See* **Echo.**

> *Economical Mate* One in which every White piece on the

board participates, with the optional exception of King and Pawns. In Problem No. 17, every mate is an economical one, except when the Black King stands on Black's QR1 in the mating position.

Mirror Mate   Occurs when *every* square in the mated King's field is unoccupied. *See* mate following 1 . . . K—B2, in Problem No. 12.

Model Mate   One which is both *pure* and *economical. See* mate following sacrifice of Queen in Problem No. 17.

Pure Mate   Occurs when each of the unblocked squares in the mated King's field is guarded by only one White piece. *See* mate following 3 Q—KN2, in Problem No. 16, which is also a *model mate.*

Set Mate   A ready mate for a prospective move by Black, such as White has for every prospective Black move in Problem No. 1.

Short Mate   Delivery of mate, in one or more variations, in *less* than the stipulated number of moves. In Problem No. 6, a 3-mover, a mate in 2 moves occurs after 1 . . . 2 P—any.

Smothered Mate   Delivery of mate to a King blocked by his own pieces. This is accomplished with a Knight. For example, place Black King on KR1, Black Rook on KN1, and Black Pawns on KR2 and KN2. The White Knight can then deliver a *smothered mate* at KB7.

MEREDITH   A chess problem position containing a total of 8 to 12 pieces—after the American composer, William Meredith (1835–1903). *See* Problem Nos. 2, 4, 5, 6, 13, 14 & 16. *See* **Decalet; Miniature.**

MINIATURE   A chess problem position containing a total of *no more* than 7 pieces. *See* Problem No. 17. *See* **Decalet; Meredith.**

MINOR DUAL   *See* **Dual.** A *minor dual* occurs when the choice of moves available to White, in response to a move by Black, does not relate to thematic or otherwise significant variations. *See* example (Problem No. 11) in definition of *dual.*

MIRROR MATE   *See* **Mate.**

MODEL MATE   *See* **Mate.**

MOVE Designates a move by *both* White and Black. In orthodox problems, however, White (obviously enough) has one move *more* than Black. For example, in a 2-mover, White moves and Black moves (accounting for one move); then White mates (accounting for the second move).

NONTHEMATIC VARIATION The line of play in a chess problem which is not related to the theme, such as the variation following 1 . . . K—N8 in Problem No. 8.

OBTRUSIVE MAN A promoted Queen, Rook, Bishop, or Knight in the *set position* of a problem.

OBTRUSIVE PIECE *See* **Obtrusive Man.**

ONE-LINER *See* **Single-Line Problem.**

ORIGINALITY The creation of a new theme or the presentation of an existing one in a uniquely novel manner.

ORIGINAL or ORIGINAL PROBLEM A chess problem published for the first time.

ORTHODOX PROBLEM *See* **Direct-Mate Problem.**

PIECE *Any* unit on the chessboard, including King, all men, and Pawns. *See* **Man.**

PURE MATE *See* **Mate.**

REFLEX MATE PROBLEM or REFLEX PROBLEM A *selfmate* problem in which *each* side *must* mate on the move if able to do so. The *reflex* condition is, of course, a severe restriction on the side charged with the task of compelling the enemy to deliver mate in a specified number of moves.

RESTRICTIVE KEY or RESTRICTIVE KEY MOVE A key move which reduces the mobility of Black, especially that of the Black King. *See* **Key Move.** *See Key Move* in *Novotny* theme problem, No. 12.

RETRACTION The taking back of a specified number of moves, the position being restored to a point *before* the moves were taken.

RETRACTOR or RETRACTOR PROBLEM A chess problem the solution of which entails retraction of a stipulated number of moves by one side or the other or both.

RETROGRADE ANALYSIS The study of a setting for the purpose of determining how it could have arisen in a regular game of chess, and whether, among other things, the position is legal, or whether certain moves are allowed in the set position, such as castling or *en passant* Pawn capture. *See* **Legal Move;** *Castling* theme; *En Passant* theme.

SECONDARY THREAT *See* **Contingent Threat.**

SELFMATE PROBLEMS or SELFMATES Chess problems in which it is stipulated that White, moving first, is to *force* Black to deliver mate to White in a specified number of moves, against any "defense." **Selfmates** are not generally considered to be *fairy problems,* being regarded to be in a class by themselves.

SET MATE *See* **Mate.**

SET PLAY The variations which could or would take place in a given setting were Black to move first instead of White. *See* Problem No. 1.

SET POSITION or SETTING The position of a chess problem as it actually appears, *before* any move is made by either side. By convention, the White side is always at the lower end of the chessboard, moving up.

SHORT MATE *See* **Mate.**

SINGLE-LINE PROBLEM or SINGLE-LINER A chess problem the solution of which consists of one and only one variation. *See* **One-Liner.** *See* Problem No. 5.

SMOTHERED MATE *See* **Mate.**

STALEMATE PROBLEMS Chess problems in which it is stipulated that one side stalemate the other in a specified number of moves, against best defense.

STAR FLIGHT *See* **Flight Square.**

SUI-MATE PROBLEMS *See* **Selfmate Problems.**

SWITCHBACK or SWITCHBACK MOVE The return of a White piece to its original position, for the purpose, say, of delivering mate —as may occur in a 2-move problem.

TASK PROBLEM or TASKER A chess problem in which the theme or idea is expressed in maximum or ultimate form, such as the *Pickaninny Task* and four-fold *Promotion Task* combined in Problem No. 14.

THEMATIC DUAL A choice of play available to White, in response to a move by Black, which *includes* a thematic variation. This is a significant flaw which, as a rule, renders the problem unsound. For example, were dual continuations available to White in Problem No. 8, after Black's Pawn moves, we would have **Thematic Duals.** *See* **Dual; Minor Dual; Major Dual.**

THEMATIC VARIATION The line of play in a chess problem which expresses the basic *theme* or idea. *See* variations following Black's Pawn moves in Problem No. 8.

THEME The idea or so-called plot of the problem requiring unique strategy to accomplish the desired end.

TRY or TRIES Basically, attempted *key moves* which fail to solve a problem. The term *try,* however, has taken on the meaning of a *key move* which *almost* works and against which the only defense is a subtle Black maneuver.

TWINS or TWIN PROBLEMS Two physically identical settings—each appearing in a different part of the chessboard; or two settings which are almost physically identical. Each of the *twins* must be solved by a different *key move,* that being a basic requisite, for the main feature, as a rule, is why a common key will not do for both.

TWO-MOVER; THREE-MOVER; ETC. An orthodox chess problem which is to be solved in two moves, three moves, etc., as specified.

UNDERPROMOTION The promotion of a Pawn to a man other than a Queen.

UNIT *See* **Piece.**

UNORTHODOX PROBLEM A chess problem in which the stipulation calls for a deliberate deviation from the standard rules and regulations governing the game of chess. *See* **Fairy Problems; Conditional Problems; Helpmate Problems; Selfmate Problems.**

UNPROVIDED CHECK A prospective check by Black with which White cannot readily cope in the set position, and by which, unless White actually provides a defense against it, the play will be prolonged and the problem will not be solved in the stipulated number of moves. It follows, therefore, that an *unprovided check* may serve as a clue to the solver who must find a key to overcome an obvious obstacle.

UNPROVIDED FLIGHT   Inability of White to deliver mate, in the event the Black King moves to an available *flight square* in the *set position*. This is of particular importance in 2-movers. *See* Problem No. 11, where the Black King's two flights cannot be met with mate in the set position.

UNSOUND PROBLEM   One that is "cooked," has no solution, or is irreparably faulty by virtue of illegality of position, thematic impurity, or other significant flaws.

WAITER   A chess problem in which the key exerts no threat but places Black in *Zugzwang*, so that any move made by Black leads to suicide. *See* Problems No. 1 and No. 7.

WHITE, ALAIN   *See* Christmas Series.

THEMES

Chess problems have been called the "poesy of chess." True enough, the inspiration which has propelled chess-problem composers to artistic creations finds its parallel in the poetry of literature.

The earliest problems, reasonably enough, arose from practical positions in the game of chess. As chess-problem composition, in the course of centuries, fired the imagination of creative minds, many themes were evolved—actual plots calling for extraordinary maneuvers. The chess problem has developed into a phase of chess quite different, apparently, from the practical game in which there is implicit but one consideration: Can I win? But since the standard rules of chess govern both the game and the orthodox chess problem, an identity of strategy employed in both is inevitable.

The strategy in many chess-problem themes is well known to chessplayers, who, however, may have no awareness that many of their tricks are the stock in trade of chess problems. The resourceful chessplayer knows the value of decoying enemy pieces (*see*

ROMAN theme; Problem No. 15); or causing interference of enemy pieces (*see* GRIMSHAW, NOVOTNY, and PLACHUTTA themes; Problem Nos. 7, 12 & 15); or ambushing enemy pieces (*see* ANNIHILATION theme; Problem No. 2); or forcing a devastating *Zugzwang* (*see* Problem No. 1); or sacrificing a piece for immediate or eventual advantage (*see* Problem No. 17). Hence, the chess problem, owing its life to the game of chess, is prepared to contribute a trick or two to the player of the game.

An alphabetical listing of the better-known themes is given below, followed by illustrative diagrams of chess problems. In some instances, earlier examples of a pioneering nature (such as Healey's BRISTOL, Problem No. 3) are given preference, although there are compositions of later years of superior construction.

Added-Mate Waiter   Problem No. 1 by William Meredith [1]

We have a block position, that is, one where White has a ready mate for *every* possible Black move. Were Black to move first, White would be all set, and it *appears* that every attempted key move by White disturbs the array. But White does find a key move which allows for *more* variations than exist in the set position, and White now *waits,* having a ready mate for every move by Black.

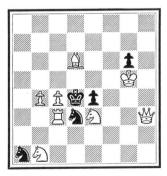

**WHITE TO PLAY AND MATE
IN 2 MOVES**

[1] *Dubuque Chess Journal,* 1886

1	Q—R5!	PxQ	2	N—B5 mate
1	. . . .	KxN	2	B—B5 mate
1	. . . .	N/R8-any	2	N—B2 mate
1	. . . .	N—K4	2	B—B5 mate
1	. . . .	N/Q6-else	2	Q—R8 mate

Ambush   *See* **Annihilation.**

Annihilation   **Problem No. 2 by Sam Loyd** [2]

Annihilation, essentially a 3-move theme, consists of initially moving a White piece along a line that *must* be cleared to a square where it can be captured. White's second move is an ambush behind the capturing Black piece. When the Black piece vacates the line, the ambushing White piece delivers mate. *See* variation following 1 . . . NxB.

Note that if it were possible physically to remove the key piece from the board, the desired end would be accomplished. That is an essential test of the *Annihilation* theme.

Annihilation employs ambush strategy as an integral part of the theme. Ambush, in and by itself, is a recognized theme, and there are many examples of merit.

**WHITE TO PLAY AND MATE
IN 3 MOVES**

1	B—B5, NxB	2	Q—R7!	N-any	3	Q—N1 mate
1	. . . . N-else	2	Q—Q7	any	3	Q—Q1 mate

[2] *Wilke's Spirit of the Times,* 1868

Bristol   **Problem No. 3 by Frank Healey** [3]

The *Bristol*, essentially a 3-move theme, entails the clearance of a line by a White piece, for the purpose of allowing the White Queen to move along the cleared line to a square contiguous to the one on which the key piece is now located. The Queen reaches the destination in two moves and delivers mate. *See* variation ending in 3 Q—N1 mate.

Note that if it were possible physically to remove the key piece from the board, the desired end would be accomplished. That is an essential test of the *Bristol* theme.

Healey's *Bristol* appeared close to 100 years ago. It was a sensational discovery, and it has served as a basis for many line-clearance ideas.

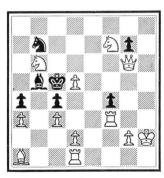

WHITE TO PLAY AND MATE
IN **3** MOVES

1	R—R1!!, B—Q2 or B—K1	2	Q—N1! B—N4	3	Q—N1 mate
		2	. . . . else	3	Q—N4 mate
1	. . . . B—B3 or B—R3	2	QxB mate or Q—B6 mate		
1	. . . . N-any	2	Q—Q6 mate		

Castling   **Problem No. 4 by P.L. Rothenberg** *after* **Alain White** [4]

By generally accepted convention, castling *is* allowed in chess,

[3] First Prize, Bristol Tourney, 1861
[4] *Chess Review*, 1942

problems, in the absence of absolute proof, in a given position, that castling is not permitted because either the King or the Rook must have moved. In Problem No. 4, the essential feature is the echo shown after 1 . . . R—Q1 and 1 . . . Castles.

Note that the Black Pawn is needed to enable Black to castle. Why? *See* solution.

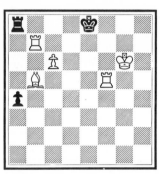

**WHITE TO PLAY AND MATE
IN 2 MOVES**

1	R(B5)—B7, threatening	2	P—B7 mate
1	. . . .	R—Q1	2	R/N7—K7 mate
1	. . . .	Castles	2	R/B7—B7 mate
1	. . . .	K—Q1	2	R—B8 mate
1	. . . .	R—N1 or R—R2	2	P—B7 or R—N8 mate
1	. . . .	else	2	P—B7 mate

NOTE: The Black Pawn is needed to legalize castling; else, Black's last move would be chargeable to either King or Rook and castling would not be allowed.

Changed Mate Waiter   *See* **Mutate.**

En Passant   **Problem No. 5 by F. Amelung** [5]

En Passant problems always entail retrograde analysis, for it must definitely be proved that the *only* last move which Black could have made is one enabling White to make the *En Passant* key move. No. 5 is a pioneering problem in which the theme is expressed with fewest possible pieces.

[5] *Duena Zeitung,* 1897

WHITE TO PLAY AND MATE
IN 2 MOVES

1   PxP e.p., K—R4   2   RxP mate

Grab   Problem No. 6 by H. D'o. Bernard [6]

The *Grab,* a 3-move theme in its simplest form, entails the capture of a mobile Black piece, in order to force Black to make a move leading to suicide. In No. 6, Black is forced to move the Pawn as soon as the Knight is captured by White, and mate follows. In problems of longer range than three moves, the *Grab* may entail the capture of more than one Black piece. *See* OPPOSITION.

In connection with Problem No. 6, *see* MUTATE.

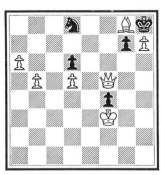

WHITE TO PLAY AND MATE
IN 3 MOVES

[6] *Observer,* 1930

1	Q—QB8,	N—B2	2	BxNch KxP	3	Q—R3 mate
1	. . . .	N—B3	2	QxN, P-any	3	Q—B3 mate
1	. . . .	N—N2	2	PxN, P-any	3	Q—B3 mate
1	. . . .	N—K3	2	QxN, P-any	3	Q—B6 mate
1	. . . .	P-any	2	Q—B3 mate		

Grimshaw   **Problem No. 7 by Sam Loyd** [7]

Mutual interference between Rook and Bishop on the same square is known as the *Grimshaw* theme. The amazing Sam Loyd's problem gives us a multiple effect, each Bishop interfering with both Rooks and each Rook interfering with both Bishops.

No. 7 also exemplifies what is known as the *Organ Pipe* theme. *Compare* NOVOTNY theme. *See* WAITER.

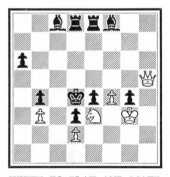

WHITE TO PLAY AND MATE
IN 2 MOVES

1 Q—R5 and White mates by 2 QxNP or 2 Q—Q5 or 2 Q—K5 or 2 N—B5, in accordance with Black's move.

Indian   **Problem No. 8 by P. A. Boorer** [8]

This, like the BRISTOL, is one of the classical themes, discovered in 1844 by an English minister, Rev. Henry A. Loveday,

[7] *Chess Monthly,* 1860
[8] *Observer,* 1938

who lived in Delhi, India—hence the name of the theme. Curiously enough, Loveday's original problem, a 4-mover, was unsound, in that it yielded to numerous key moves and a myriad of duals. Yet it remains to this day one of the greatest pioneering problems of all time.

The *Indian,* essentially a 3-move theme, entails 4 distinct elements:

    1. A White Bishop, Rook or Queen moves along a line passing a critical square.

    2. Black makes a move which leads to a stalemate of Black.

    3. White releases the stalemate by placing an interfering piece on the critical square—thus forming an indirect battery.

    4. The Black King must move into the line of the battery, and discovered mate follows, usually (but not essentially) entailing double check.

In Problem No. 8, the theme is doubled, the critical squares being White's KB6 and KN7.

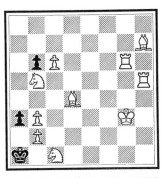

**WHITE TO PLAY AND MATE
IN 3 MOVES**

1	B—R8, P—R7	2	R—B6, KxP	3	R—B1 mate
1	. . . . PxP	2	R—N7, P—N8 (any)	3	R—R7 mate
1	. . . . K—N8	2	R—Q6ch, KxN	3	R—R1 mate
		2	. . . . K—R8	3	PxP mate

Knight Wheel   **Problem No. 9 by H. V. Tuxen** [9]

The *Knight Wheel* theme entails the employment of 8 *distinct* variations either by (a) a White Knight, in response to 8 different defenses by Black; or (b) in response to 8 different defenses by a Black Knight—as is the case in Problem No. 9. In this problem, the threat, 2 N—Q2 mate, is defeated by any move of the Black Knight, but each of the 8 moves made by the Black Knight—the maximum possible—leads to a *different* mate.

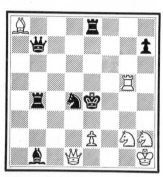

**WHITE TO PLAY AND MATE
IN 2 MOVES**

1	N—B3, threatening		2	N—Q2 mate
1	. . . .	N—B7	2	Q—Q3 mate
1	. . . .	N—N6	2	QxB mate
1	. . . .	N—N4	2	BxQ mate
1	. . . .	N—B3	2	Q—Q5 mate
1	. . . .	N—K3	2	R—K5 mate
1	. . . .	N—B4	2	R—N4 mate
1	. . . .	NxN	2	PxN mate
1	. . . .	NxP	2	QxN mate
1	. . . .	R—N7	2	QxN mate
1	. . . .	R—K4	2	RxR mate

Letter Problem   **Problem No. 10 by P. L. Rothenberg** [10]

Strictly speaking, a *Letter Problem* is not a theme, unless it

[9] *Deutsche Schachzeitung*, 1918
[10] Original (dedicated to the Macmillan Company, 1955)

happens to have thematic content. *See* RETROGRADE ANALY-SIS, below, where No. 10 is discussed.

Problem No. 10, in the faithful shape of an *M,* is dedicated to the Macmillan Company, publishers of this handbook.

It is to be noted that the mere posting of pieces on the chessboard for the purpose of constructing a setting in the shape of a letter of the alphabet can hardly be regarded as an accomplishment of merit. A *Letter Problem,* to justify its existence, must consist of pieces every one of which performs a specific function *other than* mere participation in the pictorial array. (*See* earlier discussion of economy of force, page 158.) In No. 10, such function *is* performed by every piece on the board.

WHITE TO PLAY AND MATE
IN 2 MOVES

White's missing QB accounts for the capture made by Black in the Queen's file. The Bishop must have been captured at Black's Q3 or Q5—on a black square. It follows that none of Black's 3 Pawns not situated on white squares could have arrived there via capture, since the only missing White piece is the QB. Obviously enough, Black's Pawns on QR3, Q5, and N3 could not have made the last move; nor could the Black King have moved last; nor could the Pawn at Q4 have moved from Q3, for the White King would have been in check. Therefore, the only possible last move by Black was P/Q2—Q4, and the solution follows:

$$\begin{array}{lll} 1 & \text{PxP e.p.} & \text{P—Q6} \\ 2 & \text{K—B6 mate} \end{array}$$

Miscellaneous   **Problem No. 11 by Sam Loyd** [11]

Some themes are not readily definable, for they may consist of an ingenious coup or stroke which, as a unique feature, may defy duplication. Such, essentially, is the feature of Problem No. 10, one of the most sensational compositions in existence. The "theme" of this masterpiece rests in the fantastic key move. Sam Loyd's motto for this problem was the Steinitz Gambit—intended as a hint to the solver.

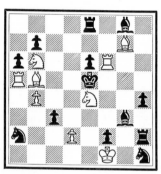

**WHITE TO PLAY AND MATE
IN 3 MOVES**

1 K—K2!!!, P—B8/Qch   2 K—K3 and White delivers mate
                                     against any defense

1 . . . .   P—B8/Nch   2 R—B2ch, KxN   3 B—Q3 mate

1 . . . .   NxP   2 B—Q3ch, N—Q4   3 R/B6-any, mate
                       2 . . . .   K—Q5   3 PxP mate

1 . . . .   KxN   2 B—Q3ch, K—Q5   3 R—B4 mate

1 . . . .   K—Q5   2 R—B4ch, P—K4   3 NxB mate

1 . . . .   else   2 K—K3 or 2 R/B6 dis ch, depending on
                                     Black's defense

[11] First Prize, *Checkmate,* 1903

Mutate   *See* **Problem No. 6 under Grab theme**

The *Mutate* is also known as the *Changed-Mate Waiter*. Essentially a two-move theme, it can be expressed in longer-range problems, as in the instant case.

We have a block position, White being ready to meet every possible Black move with a mate in the stipulated number of moves. Were Black to move first, it would be fine, and it *appears* that every attempted key move by White disturbs the setting. But White does find a key move which effects one or more changes in the set mates, and White now *waits*, having a ready continuation for every move by Black. In Problem No. 6, the set variations for 1 . . . N—B2 and 1 . . . N—B3 are changed in actual play, that being the essential element of the *Mutate*.

Problem No. 6 also employs the GRAB theme (*which see*).

Novotny   **Problem No. 12 by N. M. Gibbins** [12]

The *Novotny*, also known as the *Nowotny*, entails mutual interference between Rook and Bishop on the same square—effected by the capture of a White piece which White places on that square. *Compare* Grimshaw.

WHITE TO PLAY AND MATE
IN 2 MOVES

[12] *Leeds Mercury*, 1901

1	N—N2, RxN	2	R—B2 mate
1	. . . . BxN	2	R—Q4 mate
1	. . . . PxNch	2	R—QR4 mate
1	. . . . P—B5	2	RxP mate
1	. . . . P—N5	2	RxP mate
1	. . . . K—B2	2	R—B8 mate
1	. . . . K—K4	2	N—B4 mate
1	. . . . PxR	2	BxP mate

Opposition   **Problem No. 13 by Sam Loyd** [13]

Opposition, essentially a 3-move theme, entails a battle be-tween a White piece and a Black piece—action and counterac-tion. Ambush or forking (as in the instant problem) may be in-volved, for note how the White Queen, in hot pursuit of the Black Bishop, simultaneously attacks Black's KRP. This problem was aptly dubbed "The Love Chase" by the delightful Sam Loyd.

Note that the GRAB theme (*which see*) is a type of *Opposition.*

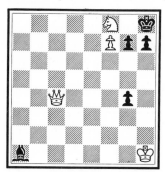

**WHITE TO PLAY AND MATE
IN 3 MOVES**

1	Q—KB1, RP—any or . . . B—N7	2	Q—QN1,° P—N3	3	QxB mate
1	. . . B—B6 or B—Q5	2	Q—Q3,° P—N3	3	QxB mate
1	. . . B—K4 or B—B3	2	Q—B5,° P—N3	3	QxB mate
1	. . . P—N6	2	N—N6ch! PxN	3	Q—R3 mate
1	. . . P/N2—any	2	QxB mate		

[13] *Leipziger Illustrated Zeitung,* 1869
° Queen threatens mate at KR7; this can be met by 2 . . . P—N3 only.

Organ Pipe   *See* **Problem No. 7 under Grimshaw theme**

Pickaninny   **Problem No. 14 by Nathan Rubens** [14]

This is a task theme. A Black Pawn is stationed on its original square, able to make 4 moves (the maximum)—single or double move forward or capture on either side. For each move of the Black Pawn, we have a distinct variation. No. 14 is an amazing achievement, for the *Pickaninny* is combined with the fourfold PROMOTION theme. White promotes to a different man, in response to each move by the Black Pawn.

The *Pickaninny* can be expressed in 2-move form.

See PROMOTION theme in connection with Problem No. 14.

WHITE TO PLAY AND MATE
IN 3 MOVES

1	PxP/K7, P—Q4	2	P—K8/Nch KxP	3	N—Q8 mate
1	. . . . PxBP	2	P—K8/B KxP	3	R—N6 mate
1	. . . . PxKP	2	P—K8/R K—B2	3	R(K8)—KB8 mate
1	. . . . P—Q3	2	P—K8/Q any	3	R—N6 or Q—B7 mate
1	. . . . KxP	2	P—K8/Qch K—B3	3	R or Q mates

Plachutta   **Problem No. 15 by Otto Wurzburg** [15]

Plachutta, essentially a 3-move theme, entails mutual inter-ference between two pieces of *similar* motion, such as Rook and

[14] *Providence Journal,* 1947
[15] *Zlata Praha,* 1909

Rook, Queen (moving laterally) and Rook, or Queen (moving diagonally) and Bishop. The Black interfering piece is forced to vacate a line, thus losing control of the line, and White promptly takes advantage of that. In Problem No. 15, one of the Black Rooks guards the Black Pawn at KN5 and the other guards Black's Q2 square. Each Rook is forced to move to Black's Q5 to meet a threat, and subsequently is forced to relinquish the line controlled by it.

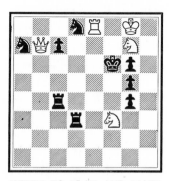

WHITE TO PLAY AND MATE
IN 3 MOVES

1	N—K5, threatening	2	Q—QN2	and	3	N—Q7 or
						NxP/N4 mate
1	.... R/B5—Q5	2	Q—Q5	RxQ	3	NxP mate
				.... else	3	N—Q7 mate
1	.... R/Q6—Q5	2	Q—K4	RxQ	3	N—Q7 mate
				.... else	3	NxP mate
1	.... R—N5	2	QxR	R—Q5	3	Q—K7 mate
				.... else	3	NxP mate
1	.... N—N4	2	Q—B6ch	N—Q3	3	N—Q7 mate
				.... RxQ	3	NxP mate
				.... R—Q3	3	N—Q7 mate
				.... N—K3	3	R or QxN mate

There are a number of technical distinctions in the *Plachutta*. No. 15 covers one phase, known as the *Wurzburg-Plachutta*.

Promotion   *See* **Problem No. 14 under Pickaninny theme**

The *Promotion* theme has many aspects. It may entail under-promotion by White, by Black, or by both; it may consist of multiple promotion by White or Black to a piece of the same rank; and it may, as in the case of Problem No. 14, involve the fourfold promotion task, one of the most ingenious accomplishments on the chessboard, entailing as it does promotion to 4 different men, in response to 4 different moves by Black. No. 14 includes the PICKANINNY theme (*which see*), and is a remarkable combination of two tasks.

Retrograde Analysis   *See* **Problem No. 10 under Letter Theme**

See definition of RETROGRADE ANALYSIS under TERMS. See also Problem No. 4.

In No. 10 we cannot find a move leading to mate in 2 until it dawns upon us to ascertain Black's last move. It is only then that we hit upon the solution.

Roman   **Problem No. 16 by J. Moeller** [16]

In the *Roman,* essentially a 3-move theme, a Black Piece, in order to meet an immediate threat by White, allows itself to be decoyed to a less advantageous square than that on which it is originally situated. White then exerts another threat which the decoyed piece can meet only by fatally affecting the Black position. In Problem No. 16, White's immediate try—1 Q—N1 (threatening 2 Q—N8 mate)—is meaningless, for Black effectively defends with 1 . . . B—N6. White, therefore, lures the Black Bishop to Black's K2, and when Black is again forced to control Black's QN1 square, the QP is shut off by the Bishop, and White is able to deliver mate along the diagonal.

[16] *Skakbladet,* 1911

**WHITE TO PLAY AND MATE
IN 3 MOVES**

1	Q—N7, threatening	2	QxP	and	3	Q—B6 mate
1	. . . . B—K2	2	Q—QN2!	B—Q3	3	Q—N2 mate
			. . . .	else	3	Q—N8 mate
1	. . . . K—N2	2	QxPch	K—R1	3	Q—B6 mate
			. . . .	K—R3	3	P—R8(R or Q)
						mate

Turton or Turton Doubling   **Problem No. 17 by Otto
                                          Wurzburg** [17]

The *Turton*, essentially a 3-move theme, entails the passage of
the key piece, a White Bishop (or Rook), over a critical square.
This square is subsequently occupied by the White Queen which
then delivers mate by moving along the line previously trans-
versed by the Bishop (or Queen). The key piece may or may not
support the Queen when mate is delivered; in No. 17, the Bishop
is needed for support of the Queen in some of the mating variations. The critical square is White's KN4.

Note the elegant sacrifice in the non-thematic variation, following 1 . . . P—R4.

[17] *British Chess Magazine,* 1896

**WHITE TO PLAY AND MATE
IN 3 MOVES**

1	B—R3, threatening	2	Q—N4	and	3	Q—B8 mate
1	. . . . P—R4	2	Q—R6ch!!	KxQ	3	B—B8 mate
			. . . .	else	3	Q—B8 mate

Underpromotion   *See* **Promotion.**

Waiter (Simple)   *See* **Problem No. 7 under Grimshaw theme**

Problem No. 7 is an incomplete block, for White has a ready mate in the set position for every Black move except 1 . . . B—KN2, 1 . . . B—R3, 1 . . . P—R4, 1 . . . R—K2, and 1 . . . R—Q3. The key move is a simple waiting maneuver enabling White to meet *every* Black move with a mate.

Note that in the simple *Waiter*, White's key move does not provide for added mates (as in the ADDED-MATE WAITER, *which see*) or changed mates (as in the MUTATE, *which see*).

In all *Waiter* problems White exerts no threat, but simply sits back comfortably after the key is made, waiting for Black to commit suicide.

In the simple *Waiter* which is of merit, thematic or otherwise, striking play must, as a rule, be incorporated. *See* GRIMSHAW theme, in connection with Problem No. 7.

BIBLIOGRAPHY

ALTSCHUL SERIES   the most beautiful limited-edition chess-problem books in existence; published (1941–1945) by Frank Altschul's Overbrook Press, Stamford, Connecticut; consisting of some nine volumes, authored (for the most part) and edited by Alain White, of which outstanding are *A Century of Two-Movers* by Alain White, Comins Mansfield, Frederick Gamage, and Vincent Eaton (1941), *A Sketchbook of American Chess Problematists* by Alain White, Edgar W. Allen, and Burney M. Marshall (1942) and *The Two-Move Chess Problem in the Soviet Union* by Alain White, Richard Cheney, and Albrecht Buschke (1943), in two volumes.

CHESS CAMEOS   *Chess Cameos* by F. Bonner Feast, David McKay Co., Philadelphia, 1936.

CHRISTMAS SERIES   authored (for the most part), edited, and published by Alain White (1905–1936); consisting of over forty volumes, of which outstanding are *Sam Loyd and His Chess Problems* by Alain C. White (1913), *The Good Companion Two-Mover* by George Hume and Alain C. White (1922) and *The Chess Problem* by H. Weenink (1926).

Composed Chess Endings

By P. L. Rothenberg

A composed chess ending is a position wherein the stipulation calls for a conclusive demonstration that a win, by a given side, can be forced against best defense; or that a draw, by a given side, can be forced against any offense.

A composed chess ending is usually referred to as an *ending*, but it is frequently called an *endgame* or an *end-game*. The latter terms, however, are more commonly applied to natural positions, i.e., those arising in actual games. Some confusion has arisen in the interchange of terms. It is best to specify, therefore, whether a given position is a *composed* or *natural* one. In using the term *ending*, we shall be referring only to composed positions.

We are here concerned only with *orthodox* composed endings, as defined above. Endings with stipulations other than those calling for a standard win or draw are not within the scope of our discussion. Such endings, embracing as they do a variety of unorthodox conditions, are more nearly related to Fairy Chess (see definition on page 163) than to the actual game of chess.

A composed ending is distinguishable from a *natural endgame* (one arising in an actual game of chess, in which a win or a draw is to be demonstrated) or a *chess problem* (one in which the composer's stipulation, in orthodox settings, calls for a mate in a specified number of moves; and in all others, the number of moves in which the condition is to be fulfilled is also almost invariably specified).

Generally, a composed ending has the following characteristics:

(a) the number of moves in which the desired end is to be accomplished is *not* specified; and (b) by convention, White is usually the side charged with accomplishing the objective. The stipulations are, therefore, generally limited to *White to Play and Win* or *White to Play and Draw*.

The following criteria are universally accepted as standards for sound composition of chess endings:

1. The composed ending must be a legal position, i.e., one which can conceivably arise in a regular game of chess.

2. The composed ending should have the appearance of a natural endgame, i.e., one *likely* to arise in a game of chess.

3. If a win is to be accomplished, White must *not* have a force or positional advantages palpably greater than or superior to those of Black; if a draw is to be attained, White should seem to be in an *apparently* hopeless position.

4. It follows, therefore, that whatever the stipulation—win or draw —the solution to an ending of merit entails unusual strategy, subtle maneuvers, surprise coups, ingenious lines of play, and the like.

5. Whereas a good key move—subtle and non-violent—is desirable, the poor quality of the key does not necessarily affect the merit of the ending. In many splendid endings, an obvious key move initiates play of an extraordinary depth and beauty. (Compare section on Chess Problems where you will find that good key moves are, as a rule, of basic importance.)

Composed endings can be subdivided into a myriad of classifications and sub-classifications, with the minutest distinctions between one ending and another painstakingly drawn. A detailed breakdown, e.g., can be found in *Collection of Chess Studies* by A. A. Troitzky (David McKay Co., 1937). The following classification is intended as a comprehensive picture, and it is, of necessity, more arbitrary than exhaustive:

THEMATIC ENDINGS

General General endings are those with a striking idea or so-called "plot" requiring unique strategy to attain the objective. The themes in endings and in chess problems are frequently identical, or, at the very least, closely related. The term "theme," however, is more often than not loosely applied to endings. It is to be noted that a genuine theme is a crystallized feature, the very heart of a composition, and it does not follow that even extraordinarily beautiful play, such as is found in Ending No. 27, is necessarily thematic. *See* Endings Nos. 1–6.

Tempo & Opposition Endings wherein tempoing, triangulation, King *vs.* King opposition or a battle of King *vs.* piece or piece *vs.* piece are employed. *See* Endings Nos. 7–10. *See* also Ending No. 20.

Domination Endings where the essential feature is *Zugzwang,* Black being forced into a fatal disadvantage by whatever move he makes, no matter how great a choice of moves may be available. *See* Ending No. 11.

Geometric Endings wherein the essential point is the competitive race between two pieces (usually King *vs.* Pawn), one moving diagonally and the other vertically, with some startling results. *See* Endings Nos. 12–14.

MATING NET or PARALYSIS Endings wherein a relentless pursuit or attack paralyzes the enemy or forces him into a position where a mate—surprising and unique, very often—is inescapable. *See* Endings Nos. 15–17.

DRAWING COUPS Endings in which White, seeking a draw, compels Black, in effect, to stalemate White; or renders Black helpless while White stalemates himself; or forces a perpetual repetition of moves. *See* Endings Nos. 18–21. *See* also Nos. 8, 9, 12, and 25.

TRICK ENDINGS Endings where an extraordinary "trick"—legal but thoroughly unexpected—must be employed in order to accomplish the desired end. *See* Ending No. 25.

PRACTICAL ENDINGS Endings specifically composed for the purpose of illustrating how a position, reasonably expected to occur in the game of chess, is to be handled. *See* Endings Nos. 22–24, but note that some of the other positions, such as the *Geometric* endings and the *Tempo* and *Opposition* endings, can offer as much practical value. There is an inevitable overlapping, and it is difficult to delineate with absolute precision what ending is *not* practical. In solving an ending, the standard rules of the game of chess are followed throughout, and in the light of the millions of permutations which occur in the game, one may well gain a practical point from *any* ending. A splendid text on practical endings is *Basic Chess Endings* by Reuben Fine (David McKay Co., 1941), who leans heavily on Kling and Horwitz, two gifted pioneers in the composition of practical endings, whose earliest works appeared during the middle of the nineteenth century.

MISCELLANEOUS   Endings where the essential line of play cannot be pinpointed with as reasonable precision as has been applied to the above-outlined features. Such endings, though without benefit of identity by nomenclature, can be fully as rich in content as their baptized brethren, if not more so. *See* Endings Nos. 26–27.

In the solutions which follow, the main line or lines of play are given. An exhaustive analysis of subvariations is, for the most part, left to the solver. This is also true of tries which in many of the positions just fall short of accomplishing the objective. All of the positions have been tested for soundness. Where a move is followed by one or more exclamation points, it may very well be the only one, or the best one, available at that point.

No. 1. Rev. Saavedra *Source?*

**BLACK TO PLAY; WHITE
TO WIN**

This is one of the great classics of all time, with underpromotion coming as a complete surprise:

1	. . . .	R—Q3ch
2	K—N5!	R—Q4ch
3	K—N4	R—Q5ch
4	K—N3	R—Q6ch
5	K—B2	R—Q5!!

If 6 P—B8/Q, R—QB5ch; 6 QxR stalemate.

| 6 | P—B8/R!!! | . . . . |

If 6 K—B3, R—Q8 and White's King must return to B2, etc.

| 6 | . . . . | R—QR5 |
| 7 | K—N3 and wins! | |

No. 2. M. S. Liburkin *Vechernaya Moscva, 1933*

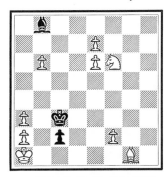

WHITE TO PLAY AND WIN

This won first prize against heavy competition. We find underpromotions ingeniously conceived by a great artist.

White is apparently in dire straits:

1	N—K4ch	K—Q6
2	N—B5ch	K—B6
3	N—N3	B—K4
4	P—B4	B—N2

5	P—K8/N	B—R1
6	P—B5	B—K4
7	B—R2!	BxB
8	P—N7	B—K4
9	P—N8/B!!	. . . .

If 9 P—N8/Q, K—B5 dis ch; 10 QxB, P—B8/Qch; 11 NxQ stalemate.

9	. . . .	BxB
10	N—B7	BxN
11	P—K7	B—K4
12	P—K8/R!!	. . . .

If 12 P—K8/Q, K—B5 dis ch; 13 QxB, P—B8/Qch; 14 NxQ stalemate.

12	. . . .	B—B3
13	R—K6	B—N2
14	P—B6 and wins	

No. 3. A. A. Troitzky Chess Studies, 1937

WHITE TO PLAY AND WIN

Troitzky is one of the immortals in the composition of chess endings. His amazing study of King and two Knights against King and Pawn remains unequaled. Here we find the Roman theme (see discussion on page 185) which entails decoying a Black piece with fatal results for Black.

1	B—K3	P—Q7
2	BxP	R—Q2ch
3	K—B6	RxB
4	K—B7	P—B8/Q
5	B—Q5ch!!	. . . .

Decoying the Rook, for if 5 . . . K—R2; 6 RxQ, K—R3; 7 K—B6, K—R4; 8 K—B5 and wins.

5	. . . .	RxB
6	RxQ	R—QR4
7	K—N6 and wins	

Exactly as in Rev. Saavedra's No. 1!

No. 4. A. A. Troitzky Chess Studies, 1937

WHITE TO PLAY AND WIN

In No. 4 the composer employs the Indian theme (page 176).

1	N—R3ch	K—R8
2	B—B3	P—R4!
3	B—B6!!	P—R5
4	N—K5	R—N3

(Or 4 . . . R—KB7.)

5   N—QB6 dis ch . . . .

(Or 5 N—KB3 dis ch.)

5	. . . .	R—N7
6	N—Q4	R—N7ch
7	K—B3	R any
8	N/Q4—B2 mate	

No. 5. E. I. Umnov Trud, 1928

WHITE TO PLAY AND WIN

The Novotny theme (see page 181) is the kernel of No. 5:

1	P—N7	B—R7
2	P—B4ch	K—R3!
3	P—K7	R—K6
4	B—K5!	. . . .

The Novotny theme!

4	. . . .	RxB
5	P—N8/Nch!!	K—N3
6	N—Q7ch and	
	wins	

No. 6. T. C. L. Kok *Tijdschrift, 1936*

WHITE TO PLAY AND WIN

The Plachutta theme, entailing the interference between two pieces of *like* motion, is found in No. 6. (For a more complete discussion of the Plachutta theme, see page 183.)

1	P—N7	B—R7!
2	R—K5ch	BxR

If 2 . . . QxR; 3 P—N8/Qch, QxQ; 4 P—R8/Qch, K—K2; 5 Q—B6ch, K—K1; 6 Q—B7ch, K—Q1; 7 Q—Q7 mate.

3	P—R8/Qch	BxQ
4	P—N8/Qch	K—K2
5	Q—B7ch	K—K1
6	Q—Q7ch	K—B1
7	Q—B7 mate	

No. 7. David Joseph *Sunday Express, 1921*

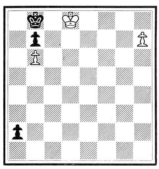

WHITE TO PLAY AND WIN

We have opposition of Queen *vs.* Queen here. The Black Queen offers herself for no altruistic reasons, for a capture would result in stalemate. Here it is particularly instructive to study the alternatives and to determine their futility.

1	P—R8/Q	P—R8/Q!
2	Q—N8!!!	Q—R7!
3	Q—K8!!	Q—R5!
4	Q—K5ch	K—R1
5	Q—R8 and wins	

No. 8. Source?

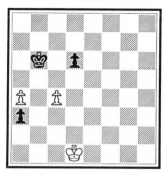

WHITE TO PLAY AND DRAW

In No. 8 we find lovely maneuvering which involves King *vs.* King opposition. The composer, unfortunately, is not known.

1	K—B2	P—R7
2	K—N2	K—R4
3	K—R1!!!	. . . .

To maintain the opposition, if Black captures the Pawn.

3	. . . .	K—N5!
4	K—N2!	P—R8/Qch
5	KxQ	KxRP
6	P—B5!	PxP
7	K—R2 and draws!	

No. 9. *M. S. Liburkin 1948*

WHITE TO PLAY AND DRAW

| 1 | K—B1 | B—B6! |

The alternative 1 . . . B—KN5 leads to the same line of play.

On the other hand, after the inferior 1 . . . B—K7 Black is unable to harass the White King.

If 1 . . . B—R5; 2 B—R5, K—N2; 3 N—B7, B—K1; 4 NxP draws.

| 2 | B—N6! | K—N2 |
| 3 | P—Q4!! | . . . . |

If now 3 . . . BxP/Q5; 4 N—B7 draws.

3	. . . .	BxPch
4	K—B2	B—Q4
5	B—B7!!	. . . .

So that if 5 . . . BxB; 6 NxB, KxN; 7 K—N3, B—B8; 8 K—B2, B—R6; 9 K—N3 and so on *ad infinitum!*

5	. . . .	B—K5ch
6	K—N3	B—B8
7	B—N6!!	B—Q4ch
8	K—B2	B—R6
9	B—B7!!!	Drawn

We are back again to the other side, Black being absolutely unable to shake off the annoying Bishop.

No. 10. N. Rossolimo *original*

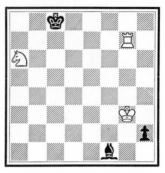

WHITE TO PLAY AND WIN

In an artistically slender setting, we find a battle between King and Knight. It is, of course, obvious that White must capture the Pawn (or stop it from queening) *and* save his Knight, in order to win.

1	R—N8ch	K—N2!
2	N—B5ch	K—N3!
3	N—R4ch	K—N4!
4	N—B3ch	K—N5!
5	N—R2ch	K—N6
6	N—B1ch	K—N7
7	KxP	KxN
8	R—N1 and wins	

No. 11. A. A. Troitzky *Tijdschrift, 1917*

WHITE TO PLAY AND WIN

Troitzky's artistry in domination is second to none.

1	B—Q4ch	K—B8
2	Q—Q1ch	K—N7!
3	Q—K2ch	K—R6!
4	Q—K4!!!	. . . .

Now the Black Queen has access to 22 squares, each move leading either to loss of Queen or immediate mate.

4	. . . .	P—K4
5	BxP	Q—N8
6	Q—B3ch	. . . .

White mates next move.

No 12. Richard Reti (version)

WHITE TO PLAY; BLACK TO DRAW

The great Reti, whose fame is primarily based on over-the-board chess, has a number of creditable endings among his choice compositions. No. 12 is one of the most famous, and it has appeared in various forms, the principal feature, of course, being retained in each. The setting of No. 12 was deliberately arranged to emphasize the similarity to the setting of No. 13. Both appear to be so very much alike, and yet they are so different.

1	P—R4	. . . .

To give Black the task of drawing at this point seems fantastic.

1	. . . .	K—N7
2	P—R5	. . . .

2 K—N3, K—B6 leads to the main line.

2	. . . .	K—B6
3	K—N3	. . . .

If 3 P—R6, K—Q7 draws.

3	. . . .	K—Q5!!
4	P—R6	. . . .

If 4 KxP, K—B4 draws!

4	. . . .	K—K6!

Black draws!

No. 13. Henri Rinck 1922

WHITE TO PLAY AND WIN

Another of the all-time greats is Henri Rinck. His works are an inexhaustible source of pleasure. No. 13 should be studied in connection with No. 12.

1	P—R4	K—N6
2	P—R5	K—B6

Or 2 . . . K—B5; 3 P—R6, K—Q6; 4 P—R7, P—B7; 5
P—R8/Q, P—B8/Q; 6 Q—R6ch winning.

3	K—N1	K—Q5!
4	P—R6	K—K6
5	K—B1 and wins	

No. 14. I. A. Horowitz 1924

WHITE TO PLAY AND WIN

A splendid geometric conception:

1	K—K7	P—K5

If 1 . . . P—R7; 2 K—Q6, P—K5; 3 K—B5 and wins.

2	K—Q6	P—K6
3	K—B5	P—R7!
4	K—N4!!	P—K7

If 4 . . . P—R8/Q; 5 RxQ, KxR; 6 K—B3 wins.

5	R—K7	P—R8/Q
6	RxPch	K—N8
7	R—K1ch and wins	

No. 15. A. K. Sarytschev Chess in U.S.S.R., 1935

WHITE TO PLAY AND WIN

1	P—R6	B—Q5
2	KxB	N—N5
3	P—R7	N—B3ch
4	K—B5	NxP
5	K—N6	N—B1ch
6	K—B7	N—K2

The only way to save the Knight.

> 7   N—Q6 mate!

No. 16. K. A. L. Kubbel Schachmatny Listok, 1929

WHITE TO PLAY AND WIN

And yet another giant—Kubbel!

1	B—R5ch	K—Q3
2	P—R7	N—K2
3	K—N5	N—N3
4	KxN	P—Q7
5	P—R8/Q	B—Q6ch
6	K—B7	P—Q8/Q
7	Q—Q4 mate!	

No. 17. A. P. *Gulayev Chess in U.S.S.R., 1940*

WHITE TO PLAY AND WIN

1	P—N7	P—B7
2	B—K7!	P—B8/Q
3	B—B6	QxB
4	PxR/Qch	QxQ
5	P—Q4!!	Black is paralyzed.

No. 18. J. *Sehwers 1000 Endgames, 1910*

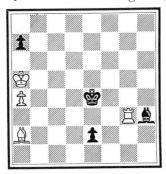

WHITE TO PLAY AND DRAW

1	B—Q5ch	K—Q5!
2	R—N1	B—B8
3	R—N4ch	KxB
4	R—N4!	P—K8/R!
5	R—N1!	RxR
	Stalemate!	

No. 19. H. Mattison Deutsches Wochenschach, 1918

WHITE TO PLAY AND DRAW

1	R—Q7	R—Q7
2	P—N7	N—K5ch
3	K—B3	B—R2
4	P—N8/Qch	BxQ
5	R—QN7	N—N4ch
6	K—N4	R—N7ch
7	K—B5	B—R7
8	R—N7ch!!	KxR
	Stalemate	

No. 20. K. A. L. Kubbel *Koelnische Volkszeitung, 1926*

WHITE TO PLAY AND DRAW

The great Kubbel in usual form!

1	P—K7	B—N1
2	P—K5	BxP
3	B—Q7	B—Q3ch
4	K—R4!	BxP
5	B—K6ch	K—R1
6	B—Q5!!	Drawn

The White Bishop continues to offer himself at QB4, Q5, or K6; Black dare not capture, for stalemate follows; and so the dance continues forever!

No. 21. T. C. L. Kok *1933*

WHITE TO PLAY AND DRAW

| | 1 | R—B2ch | K—R8 |

If the Black King moves to the sixth rank, White can stalemate himself (by 2 R—B3ch and 3 R—KR3, followed by 4 R—R5 and 5 P—R4).

2	R—B3	P—N6
3	R—R3	P—N7
4	R—R3ch	K—N8
5	RxP	K—B7
6	R—B4ch	K—N6
7	R—B8	P—N8/Q
8	R—N8ch	K—B7
9	RxQ	KxR
10	P—R4	. . . .

And now White shuffles to his heart's content between N5 and R5; if Black captures the Bishop Pawn, White is stalemated!

No. 22. Sam Loyd American Chess-Nuts, 1868

WHITE TO PLAY AND DRAW

The amazing Sam Loyd finds a bit of humor in an ending which forcefully illustrates the inability of the Knight to gain a move:

| | 1 | B—Q7 | . . . . |

Note that 1 B—B6ch at once will *not* do.

1	. . . .	P—R7
2	B—B6ch	K—N8
3	B—R1!	KxB
4	K—B2	Drawn!

No. 23. Horowitz and Kashdan Chess Review, 1933

WHITE TO PLAY AND WIN

1	N—N3!	K—B5
2	N—R1!	K—Q6
3	K—K7	K—Q7
4	K—Q6	K—B8

If 4 . . . P—R4; 5 K—B5!, P—R5; 6 K—N4, K—B8; 7 K—R3, K—N8; 8 N—N3, PxN; 9 KxP and wins.

5	P—N4	K—N7
6	K—B6!!	. . . .

If 6 K—B5?, K—B6 draws.

6	. . . .	K—B6
7	K—B5!	K—N7
8	K—N6	K—B6
9	N—B2	KxN
10	KxP and wins	

No. 24. E. B. Cook *American Chess-Nuts, 1868*

WHITE TO PLAY AND DRAW

1	K—K7	N—N3ch
2	K—Q6	K—R6
3	K—B5	N—K4
4	P—B8/N	N—Q6ch
5	K—B4	KxP
6	N—Q7	P—N6
7	N—N6	P—N7
8	N—R4	N—K4ch
9	K—Q5	Drawn

For the Pawn falls at once or when promoted to anything but a useless Knight.

No. 25. P. L. Rothenberg *original*

WHITE TO PLAY AND DRAW

White appears to be in a hopelessly lost position, but . . .

1	RxPch	NxR
2	B—B5ch	N—K2!
3	Castles ch!!	. . . .

The miracle!

3	. . . .	B—B6
4	RxBch	QxR
5	BxNch	BxB
6	P—Q8/Qch	BxQ
	Stalemate!	

A stormy session throughout, but a bit of violence to save one's life should be excused.

No. 26. Source?

WHITE TO PLAY AND WIN

1	K—N3!!	P—B8/Q

If 1 . . . K—B3; 2 R/N5—KR5 wins.

2	R—N7ch	K—Q3

Black's King must keep out of the Queen Bishop file.

3	R—R6ch	K—Q4

Black loses at once if he captures the Rook.

4	R—N5ch	K—Q5
5	R—R4ch	K—Q6
6	R—N3ch	K—Q7
7	RxPch and wins	

Now we see the reason for the lovely key move.

No. 27. L. Ehrlich Wiener Schachzeitung, *1928*

WHITE TO PLAY AND WIN

No. 27 is a truly miraculous creation. The numerous pitfalls keep White in a dither, until victory is finally assured. The solver will find much pleasure in determining why so many seemingly acceptable moves do *not* work.

| 1 | P—B7! | R—R4ch |

Now, believe it or not, White has one move, and one move only, to save the day:

2	K—B4!!	R—R8
3	B—B6	R—B8ch
4	K—Q5!	. . . .

If 4 K—N5, R—N8ch and 5 . . . R—N1!!! draws.

4	. . . .	R—Q8ch
5	K—K6	R—K8ch
6	K—B7	R—B8ch
7	K—N7	R—N8ch

If now 8 K—R8, R—QN8; 9 P—B8/Q, R—N1 draws.

| 8 | K—R7! and wins | |

How to Promote and Organize a Chess Club*

By Samuel A. Collins

Chess speaks a universal language. In every community there are always some persons who know how to play this fascinating game. In many instances clubs have been organized and the players enjoy their many evenings together.

In the communities where clubs have not been organized, the men usually meet at each other's homes or at their places of employment. In these instances the point lacking is "interest." There may be an element of interest for a time, and then it peters out, with the result that the community is deprived of its opportunity to take its place in the world of chess.

Where there is a group of men who play at each other's homes every effort should be made to foster chess interest.

In all groups, no matter how small, there is always one member of leadership ability. It should fall upon his shoulders to try to organize a chess club. It may be difficult in the beginning, but steady effort usually results in a fine group.

In order for a chess club to survive the obstacles to growth in its earlier stages, a well thought out program to foster interest as its keynote, and a constitution to guide it, are of the utmost im-

* From *American Chess Federation Yearbook, 1940.* Reprinted by permission of the United States Chess Federation, successor to the American Chess Federation.

portance. The following bylaws may serve as a model for use in a new chess club.

CHESS CLUB CONSTITUTION

Article I. Name

The name of this organization shall be the . . . Chess Club.

Art. II. Objectives

The objectives of this organization shall be—
1. To promote the popularity of the game of chess.
2. To conduct leagues and tournaments.
3. To arrange matches with other clubs.
4. To provide entertainment and social life for members of the club.

Art. III. Membership

Anyone shall be eligible for membership, providing three-fourths of the membership shall vote favorably upon the application for membership.

Art. IV. Election of Officers and Directors

The members of the club shall elect from among their number a President, Vice-President, and Secretary-Treasurer. These officers shall also constitute the Board of Directors.

The election of officers shall take place at the first regular meeting during the month of . . .

Should a vacancy occur between elections, it shall be filled by the majority vote of the members for candidates nominated therefor.

Art. V. Duties of Officers and Directors

Section 1. The President shall—
1. Preside at all business meetings of the Club.
2. Preside at the meetings of the Board of Directors.
3. Appoint all committees.

Sec. 2. The duties of the Vice-President shall be—
1. To assist the President.
2. To preside at the meetings in the absence of the President.

Sec. 3. The duties of the Secretary-Treasurer shall be—
1. To keep the minutes of all meetings.
2. To carry on the correspondence of the Club.
3. To collect any authorized membership fees or assessments.
4. To furnish a financial statement to the Board of Directors and the members at any meeting.
5. To make such disbursements as are authorized by the Board of Directors.

Sec. 4. The duties of the Board of Directors shall be—
1. To formulate a program of chess promotion for the season.
2. To supervise the work of all committees.

Art. VI. Fees and Dues

Annual membership fee of this club shall be . . . Special assessments for any particular events may be made upon a vote of three-fourths of the entire membership.

Art. VII. Meetings

Regular monthly meetings of the members shall be held throughout the year on such day and at such place as shall be decided by the membership.

Meetings may be adjourned immediately upon call to order if there is no business of importance, in order to facilitate social, tournament, or league play. The Board of Directors may meet at any time and any place upon call of the President.

Art. VIII. Amendments

This constitution may be changed or amended by a two-thirds vote of the entire membership.

The purpose of a chess club is to furnish everyone interested in chess with an opportunity to learn, play or improve his game of chess, in the most interesting manner possible. Clubs which fail to adopt such a program are usually short lived, and the task of reorganizing is a difficult one. Dull meetings soon take toll of the membership and the existence of the club depends upon the providing of a program sufficiently attractive to hold old members and attract new ones.

In all chess organizations there are groups of interested, prospective new members. By "new" is meant those who show an interest in the game but do not know how to play. They stand about and watch a game in progress and wish they too could learn to play. It is this group that requires special attention.

The task of handling beginners should be given to a member with some teaching ability. He does not have to be the best player in the group, but one who knows the game and has the necessary patience and tact for the proper guidance of a group of learners. The ability to anticipate the needs and feelings of a student goes a long way toward holding a large percentage of these learners interested enough to continue and eventually become active members of the club. Most plans for the instruction of beginners bring the student from a general knowledge of the men and their movements on into a discussion of the more popular openings, the middle game, and the endgame. Once the student has learned the moves it is considered best to devote the major portion of the instruction period to actual play. Never hurry the progress of the student even if he seems to be taking more time than was anticipated. Let the student learn the game naturally and easily rather than under forced conditions.

Although this phase of the chess club is very important, it plays only a small part in the success of a chess club. Other activities must at all times be on the program. An important activity is the championship tournament. In a tournament each man is pitting his skill against all other entrants in his section in an effort to come out on top. Tournament chess is taken much more seriously, since competition is very keen and a mismove in one game may lose the championship. Having once played match chess, the average enthusiast of the game declines to play "skittles," as the latter brand of chess encourages shoddy play.

Club tourneys are essential in the development of a ladder system, whereby it is possible to place the members according to their respective strengths. This serves as a guide when arranging men for a team match. City and county tourneys, as they cover more territory, will attract more interest as well as players. They serve also as additional stimulus in building up a club roster.

Class tourneys are also important. No matter what the tournament may be, the fact remains that a system of segregating players of equal strength into their own class is advisable. The loss of too many games by any one player proves discouraging in most instances and is one reason for the loss of members. It is human nature to want to win, and by having section champions, more men have a chance to win recognition and a compelling desire to qualify for the next highest division remains as an incentive when the time comes for the succeeding tourney.

Consultation matches are another activity that tend to test the ability of members. The pairing of promising beginners with a stronger player is good practice. This type of play need not be restricted to those who are learning. All may join in and enjoy a consultation match. The exchange of ideas in these matches often leads the players into new avenues of experience.

Correspondence chess and exhibitions and lectures by leading experts are other activities of a progressive chess club. Nationally known experts are always available to chess clubs for exhibitions. Members thrill at the opportunity of playing with experts and exhibitions are great drawing cards for prospective members of chess clubs. The publicity and added memberships often repay the outlay necessary in having such exhibitions.

In conclusion, for a club to succeed, dramatize your meetings. You not only maintain and hold the interest of your club members, but you fire the interest of outsiders and prospective members. Appoint a publicity director who can write interesting copy. Not a week should pass without some news release. Have something new and novel all the time. That's what makes a club go.

How to Run a
Chess Tournament

By W. Ritson Morry *

The first international chess tournament in London in 1851 was a quaint affair by modern organizational standards. It was played on a knock-out system, there was no fixed day-by-day timetable, and it took several months to complete. Also there were no clocks and so the players had as much time as they needed for thought, a situation which naturally led to abuses of good sportsmanship and a lot of subsequent recrimination.

I mention this merely to show that the work of running a chess tournament is not a mere matter of getting a few competitors and seating them at boards to work out their own arrangements. It has to be planned, and the modern congress or club program has to be worked out on a businesslike basis to fit in with the increased tempo at which we all live today.

There are three main systems for running a tournament now in use, namely the knock-out, the round robin, and finally the Swiss, which really represents a combination of the best features of the knock-out with the framework of the round robin.

The purpose of this article is to show how the various systems should be applied to the arrangement of the ordinary local or club tournament, but naturally they can be similarly used for any kind of competition.

* From *1953 Year Book of the British Chess Federation*. Reprinted by permission.

1. THE KNOCK-OUT

There is little need to dwell on this system, which is extremely easy to work because all rounds are drawn from a hat and beaten players drop out until there is only one unbeaten player left. It is as simple as that.

Unfortunately, its very simplicity makes it the most unsuitable way of running a test of skill such as a chess championship ought to be. One mistake is enough to ruin the chances of any player and it frequently happens that the strongest competitor is momentarily caught off balance and a weaker player disposes of him.

There is, however, a worse defect than this from the organizer's point of view, and this is that it becomes necessary to replay drawn games and if two players start a bout of drawing with each other they can seriously disorganize the timetable.

Finally, the fact that once a player is knocked out he has no further interest in the tournament is bad from a club organizer's angle because in the later stages of the competition there are so many excluded that there is nothing to draw them to the club and attendances tend to fall away. Such a tendency can, if allowed to go unchecked, lead to the club's demise.

2. THE ROUND-ROBIN SYSTEM

As a test of skill this system is all that could be desired, for every player meets each of the competitors once (it is better still if two games each can be played with alternating colors), and a much fairer idea is gained as to the respective merits of the contenders. Moreover, drawn games do not have to be replayed and if there is a tie for the championship title this does not have to be resolved until after the main tournament is finished and so a round-by-round timetable can be worked out well in advance to fit in with other club activities.

The only defect in the system is that it is usually not possible to include more than a dozen or so players in such a tournament and in a club championship this can lead to injustices and a cooling of interest among those who think they have been wrongly omitted. To meet this, many organizers resort to a system of dividing the entries into small round-robin sections with a final round robin between the leaders; but this again leads to the danger that a strong player may be unduly penalized by an early loss in a strong subsection whilst weaker players reach the final stage from an easier subsection.

3. THE SWISS SYSTEM

In the last few years this system has become increasingly popular, and although it has at times been severely criticized in the chess press for both its real and imaginary disadvantages, it is undoubtedly the best way to run any kind of club championship for the following reasons:

1. It allows a single tournament to be run in the club in which all members can take part and thus improves the social atmosphere.

2. It allows a young or unknown player the chance to come to the fore if he is really good, without the discouragement of being omitted from the principal tournament until he has worked his way through one or more seasons of qualifying sections. I have seen many cases where players have lost interest and left clubs where they felt they were being unnecessarily subjected to this process.

3. It prevents the old hand from monopolizing a place to which he considers himself still entitled and from which no tactful secretary dares to uproot him.

In my view these advantages greatly outweigh any slight theoretical defects which a purist might urge exist in the Swiss.

One warning must be uttered here to the overenthusiastic organizer: *Do not expect the Swiss to do more than it is capable of doing.* In the early stages it was not realized that there are important limitations to the number of competitors that even this system will cover. These limitations must be respected if a satisfactory result is to be obtained.

NUMBER OF ROUNDS

Usually it is desired to achieve a reasonably accurate placing of the first three of four competitors, and to do this extra rounds are necessary beyond the number required to establish the leader. The latter will, theoretically, be clear of the field in the number of rounds required in a knock-out tournament of the same number of players. Two additional rounds are required for each additional placing wanted. Thus we can establish two complimentary rules for the guidance of the organizer:

(a) *To settle the number of rounds for a given number of players and places:* The number of rounds for a knock-out of the same number of players plus twice the number of additional placings required gives the *minimum* number of rounds required. *e.g.*—We have to cater for 32 players and want the first 4 placings. The number of rounds for a knock-out would be 5. Therefore the number of rounds which must be played is 5 plus 2 times 3, or 11.

(b) *To settle the number of players who may be admitted to ensure a given number of placings in a fixed number of rounds:* The number of rounds minus twice the number of additional placings required gives a figure which is equivalent to the number of rounds which the number of players we wish to know would require to complete a knock-out tournament. *e.g.*—We have time for 9 rounds and want three placings accurate. 9 minus 2 times 2 gives 5. This is the number of rounds in which up to 32 players could complete a knock-out. Therefore we can admit up to 32 players.

If these rules are not observed it is unreasonable to expect a fair result. There is, however, no objection to playing more than the minimum number of rounds or admitting less than the maximum number of players. In either case the efficiency of the system is increased.

PAIRINGS

Having settled the number of rounds, it is then important to arrange the program so that reasonable time is given for the completion of all games in one round before the next is paired. Indeed, the pairings have to be settled at the end of each round and unless the results are all known it is difficult and frequently impossible to make a proper pairing for the next round. Therefore, you must have rules which require the completion of games and my own practice is to give a fortnight at least for the playing of each round. Players who cannot keep to this schedule should not enter in the first place.

To control the tournament the organizer will require three things:

1. PAIRING CARDS. These should take the form shown below. They are self-explanatory and show the player's opponents in each round, his color, result, and progressive score. The organizer keeps them up to date at the end of each round.

2. PAIRING NOTICES. These can be duplicated or printed and inform the player of his opponent in each round together with his color and the date by which he must report the result.

3. WALL CHART. This must be in a form which shows each player's opponent round by round with his color, result, and progressive score.

The pairing is the most important part of the control process. This requires a certain amount of skill, but once mastered it is not very difficult. The pairing cards will be found to be most useful both in avoiding pairing the same players twice and in arranging the colors. With the aid of these cards I have found it quite easy to pair thirty or forty players in a lightning tournament within three minutes, but normally this speed is quite unnecessary and the less practiced operator will require much more time.

For the first round it is usual to draw exactly as in the case of a knock-out pairing, but there are two alternatives which some controllers think add a little to the efficiency of the system. The

SPECIMEN PAIRING CARD

NAME..					NO. ....
COMPETITION...................................					
ROUND NUMBER	COLOR	OPPONENT'S NUMBER	RESULT (1, ½, OR 0)	PROGRESSIVE TOTAL	SONNEBORN-BERGER SCORE
1					
2					
3					
4					
5					
6					
7					
8					
9					
10					
11					

first is to seed the players into two equal sections of "strong" and "weak" players and to pair a strong with a weak one in each game. The second is to pair all the strong players among themselves and all the weak players among themselves. I am not at all convinced that either of these devices achieves any tangible result and the beginner may safely ignore them for simplicity.

After the first round the pairing is controlled by the rule that players with the same score must be paired together as far as possible. Thus in pairing for round two, we divide the cards into three groups: Scores of 1, scores of ½, and scores of 0. The scores of 1 are paired together, colors being reversed from those the players had in their first-round games. The ½'s and the 0's are similarly paired within themselves but it is sometimes necessary to overlap where, for instance, there is an odd number of players with 1 or 0. In such cases one of the higher group is paired with one from the next lower group.

In the pairing for round three, the process is again repeated, but this time there will be groups ranging from 2 to 0 at half-point intervals and each group will be paired within itself with odd players dipping to the next lower group. For example, say there are seven with 2, six with 1½, and six with 1. Six of the 2's will be interpaired and the other will be paired with a 1½. Four of the remaining 1½'s will be interpaired and the other will pair with a 1. Likewise four of the 1's will play each other and the other will play a ½.

The arrangement will continue until the round which would be the final of the knock-out for the number of competitors in the tournament has been played. By this time it will be seen that there can only be one player left with a clean score, and there will also be only one with 0. Of course in practice there are likely to be no clean scores by this time since draws may have spoiled everybody's score. In either case it will no longer be possible to pair the leader or leaders with players of the same score, in the first case because there is no such opponent available and in the second because the two leaders will have played each other and drawn.

The same situation will arise at the bottom end also. The rule then is that these players must play the nearest possible opponents to them and they must have first choice of opponents even though it means that two players with the same score who would normally expect to meet must be split to make this possible. As the tournament progresses it may be that the leader will have to meet the fourth, fifth or sixth player below him (because he has played all the others nearer to him), and the same will begin to apply to other leading scorers. The rule must be to pair the leader first, then the second, then the third until you have reached the main groups which will still be found to interpair fairly easily. Then go to the bottom and deal with the tail-enders similarly. The middle groups are always done last as they never give much trouble.

This covers the rule for pairing, but we have yet to say something about colors. As far as possible, colors should be alternate, but this cannot always be done. Do not then fall into the trap I have seen so many beginners fail to avoid. Instead of pairing groups they start pairing players of one group with those of a lower group just to keep the colors right. Nothing could do more to upset the tournament and make the result unreliable. In such cases I have a rule which I always follow:

In pairing a group, I divide the cards into two sets: those wanting White and those wanting Black. I pair as many of these as possible but if there is a preponderance of one set left, I pair the remainder and toss for color.

If I have to pair two people with different scores who both want the same color, I always give the lower score White. This is done merely to give the underdog a chance. Usually the higher scorers tend to have had more Whites than Blacks because of the slight advantage White always has as between players of even strength. My method tends to correct this tendency and thus color allocation is not allowed to get worse and worse.

When a player has the same color twice running, he will have a prior claim to readjustment in the next round or rounds and should be dealt with first in the pairing of his group. A little care in this important matter pays dividends to the good organizer and a fair amount of practical experience is the only way to become expert.

It is much easier to reach a fair color distribution in an odd number of rounds than it is in an even number, and for this reason it is wiser to provide for 7, 9, 11, or 13 rounds to be played than for 8, 10, 12, or 14.

One other point requires a word of explanation. Whilst all games should be played before any round is paired, it is sometimes necessary, because of a long adjourned game, to pair with a result missing. In this case two courses may be adopted:

1. The position can be provisionally adjudicated and the expected result penciled on the players' cards until the actual result is known.

2. The game may be provisionally counted as drawn and the cards adjusted when the actual result is known.

Personally, I prefer the first method and always use it since I find it causes a smaller proportion of error if the "adjudication" is expertly done. It should also be remembered that an error from this cause is less serious in the middle or bottom of the table than it is at the top, and the leading players should never be paired if it can possibly be avoided when there is an unfinished game.

How to Make Up
Tournament Pairings*

Tournament play is the lifeblood of a chess club. It is therefore essential for club officials to know how to pair players in a tournament—to know in what order opponents meet each other, and which one plays the White pieces.

The following tables show the tournament pairings for tournaments with up to twenty players. The contestants draw numbers by lot. The number of entrants tells you which table to use.

After selecting the proper table, read the top line from left to right for first-round pairings. The first named of each pair has White. Follow the same procedure for the remaining rounds.

If there is an odd number of players, the highest number in the table indicates the bye. Thus, in a tournament with eleven players, whoever is paired with No. 12 has a bye in that round.

* From *Chess Review,* 1952. Reprinted by permission.

PAIRING TABLES

for from 3 to 20 Players

TABLE A
3 or 4 Players

RD.	PAIRINGS	
1	1:4	2:3
2	4:3	1:2
3	2:4	3:1

TABLE B
5 or 6 Players

RD.	PAIRINGS		
1	1:6	2:5	3:4
2	6:4	5:3	1:2
3	2:6	3:1	4:5
4	6:5	1:4	2:3
5	3:6	4:2	5:1

TABLE C—7 or 8 Players

RD.	PAIRINGS			
1	1:8	2:7	3:6	4:5
2	8:5	6:4	7:3	1:2
3	2:8	3:1	4:7	5:6
4	8:6	7:5	1:4	2:3
5	3:8	4:2	5:1	6:7
6	8:7	1:6	2:5	3:4
7	4:8	5:3	6:2	7:1

TABLE D—9 or 10 Players

RD.	PAIRINGS				
1	1:10	2:9	3:8	4:7	5:6
2	10:6	7:5	8:4	9:3	1:2
3	2:10	3:1	4:9	5:8	6:7
4	10:7	8:6	9:5	1:4	2:3
5	3:10	4:2	5:1	6:9	7:8
6	10:8	9:7	1:6	2:5	3:4
7	4:10	5:3	6:2	7:1	8:9
8	10:9	1:8	2:7	3:6	4:5
9	5:10	6:4	7:3	8:2	9:1

TABLE E—11 or 12 Players

RD.	PAIRINGS					
1	1:12	2:11	3:10	4:9	5:8	6:7
2	12:7	8:6	9:5	10:4	11:3	1:2
3	2:12	3:1	4:11	5:10	6:9	7:8
4	12:8	9:7	10:6	11:5	1:4	2:3
5	3:12	4:2	5:1	6:11	7:10	8:9
6	12:9	10:8	11:7	1:6	2:5	3:4
7	4:12	5:3	6:2	7:1	8:11	9:10
8	12:10	11:9	1:8	2:7	3:6	4:5
9	5:12	6:4	7:3	8:2	9:1	10:11
10	12:11	1:10	2:9	3:8	4:7	5:6
11	6:12	7:5	8:4	9:3	10:2	11:1

TABLE F—13 or 14 Players

RD.	PAIRINGS						
1	1:14	2:13	3:12	4:11	5:10	6:9	7:8
2	14:8	9:7	10:6	11:5	12:4	13:3	1:2
3	2:14	3:1	4:13	5:12	6:11	7:10	8:9
4	14:9	10:8	11:7	12:6	13:5	1:4	2:3
5	3:14	4:2	5:1	6:13	7:12	8:11	9:10
6	14:10	11:9	12:8	13:7	1:6	2:5	3:4
7	4:14	5:3	6:2	7:1	8:13	9:12	10:11
8	14:11	12:10	13:9	1:8	2:7	3:6	4:5
9	5:14	6:4	7:3	8:2	9:1	10:13	11:12
10	14:12	13:11	1:10	2:9	3:8	4:7	5:6
11	6:14	7:5	8:4	9:3	10:2	11:1	12:13
12	14:13	1:12	2:11	3:10	4:9	5:8	6:7
13	7:14	8:6	9:5	10:4	11:3	12:2	13:1

TABLE G—15 or 16 Players

RD.	PAIRINGS							
1	1:16	2:15	3:14	4:13	5:12	6:11	7:10	8:9
2	16:9	10:8	11:7	12:6	13:5	14:4	15:3	1:2
3	2:16	3:1	4:15	5:14	6:13	7:12	8:11	9:10
4	16:10	11:9	12:8	13:7	14:6	15:5	1:4	2:3
5	3:16	4:2	5:1	6:15	7:14	8:13	9:12	10:11
6	16:11	12:10	13:9	14:8	15:7	1:6	2:5	3:4
7	4:16	5:3	6:2	7:1	8:15	9:14	10:13	11:12
8	16:12	13:11	14:10	15:9	1:8	2:7	3:6	4:5
9	5:16	6:4	7:3	8:2	9:1	10:15	11:14	12:13
10	16:13	14:12	15:11	1:10	2:9	3:8	4:7	5:6
11	6:16	7:5	8:4	9:3	10:2	11:1	12:15	13:14
12	16:14	15:13	1:12	2:11	3:10	4:9	5:8	6:7
13	7:16	8:6	9:5	10:4	11:3	12:2	13:1	14:15
14	16:15	1:14	2:13	3:12	4:11	5:10	6:9	7:8
15	8:16	9:7	10:6	11:5	12:4	13:3	14:2	15:1

TABLE H—17 or 18 Players

RD.	PAIRINGS								
1	1:18	2:17	3:16	4:15	5:14	6:13	7:12	8:11	9:10
2	18:10	11:9	12:8	13:7	14:6	15:5	16:4	17:3	1:2
3	2:18	3:1	4:17	5:16	6:15	7:14	8:13	9:12	10:11
4	18:11	12:10	13:9	14:8	15:7	16:6	17:5	1:4	2:3
5	3:18	4:2	5:1	6:17	7:16	8:15	9:14	10:13	11:12
6	18:12	13:11	14:10	15:9	16:8	17:7	1:6	2:5	3:4
7	4:18	5:3	6:2	7:1	8:17	9:16	10:15	11:14	12:13
8	18:13	14:12	15:11	16:10	17:9	1:8	2:7	3:6	4:5
9	5:18	6:4	7:3	8:2	9:1	10:7	11:16	12:15	13:14
10	18:14	15:13	16:12	17:11	1:10	2:9	3:8	4:7	5:6
11	6:18	7:5	8:4	9:3	10:2	11:1	12:17	13:16	14:15
12	18:15	16:14	17:13	1:12	2:11	3:10	4:9	5:8	6:7
13	7:18	8:6	9:5	10:4	11:3	12:2	13:1	14:17	15:16
14	18:16	17:15	1:14	2:13	3:12	4:11	5:10	6:9	7:8
15	8:18	9:7	10:6	11:5	12:4	13:3	14:2	15:1	16:17
16	18:17	1:16	2:15	3:14	4:13	5:12	6:11	7:10	8:9
17	9:18	10:8	11:7	12:6	13:5	14:4	15:3	16:2	17:1

TABLE I—19 or 20 Players

RD.	PAIRINGS									
1	1:20	2:19	3:18	4:17	5:16	6:15	7:14	8:13	9:12	10:11
2	20:11	12:10	13:9	14:8	15:7	16:6	17:5	18:4	19:3	1:2
3	2:20	3:1	4:19	5:18	6:17	7:16	8:15	9:14	10:13	11:12
4	20:12	13:11	14:10	15:9	16:8	17:7	18:6	19:5	1:4	2:3
5	3:20	4:2	5:1	6:19	7:18	8:17	9:16	10:15	11:14	12:13
6	20:13	14:12	15:11	16:10	17:9	18:8	19:7	1:6	2:5	3:4
7	4:20	5:3	6:2	7:1	8:19	9:18	10:17	11:16	12:15	13:14
8	20:14	15:13	16:12	17:11	18:10	19:9	1:18	2:7	3:6	4:5
9	5:20	6:4	7:3	8:2	9:1	10:19	11:18	12:17	13:16	14:15
10	20:15	16:14	17:13	18:12	19:11	1:10	2:9	3:8	4:7	5:6
11	6:20	7:5	8:4	9:3	10:2	11:1	12:19	13:18	14:17	15:16
12	20:16	17:15	18:14	19:13	1:12	2:11	3:10	4:9	5:8	6:7
13	7:20	8:6	9:5	10:4	11:3	12:2	13:1	14:19	15:18	16:17
14	20:17	18:16	19:15	1:14	2:13	3:12	4:11	5:10	6:9	7:8
15	8:20	9:7	10:6	11:5	12:4	13:3	14:2	15:1	16:19	17:18
16	20:18	19:17	1:16	2:15	3:14	4:13	5:12	6:11	7:10	8:9
17	9:20	10:8	11:7	12:6	13:5	14:4	15:3	16:2	17:1	18:19
18	20:19	1:18	2:17	3:16	4:15	5:14	6:13	7:12	8:11	9:10
19	10:20	11:19	12:8	13:7	14:6	15:5	16:4	17:3	18:2	19:1

How a Rating System Works[*]

Systems of rating players are a great spur to competition and healthy growth. In 1950 the United States Chess Federation explained its national rating system in this way:

Rating lists will be published twice each year: as of July 31 and December 31. The first list covers 2306 players, whose ratings have been determined from 582 tournaments covering a 30-year period.

All classes of tournaments (city, club, state, district, national) will be rated, the only limitations being that the events must be either round-robin or Swiss system and run 5 or more rounds. Proper rating forms may be obtained from Mr. Montgomery Major, 123 North Humphrey Avenue, Oak Park, Illinois. At present, only tournament competition entitles a player to a rating, but it is hoped, in the near future, to include team and individual matches under the system.

The rating system is completely mathematical in its operation and measures failures as well as successes for those rated. It places no premium on inactivity, as a player must participate in at least one rated tournament every three years in order to be rated.

A player competing in a rated tournament earns a performance rating in accordance with his score in that tournament. At the end of each year, his cumulative average rating is computed; it is this rating that is published in the rating lists. In computing the average rating, a player's performance ratings and his previous

° From *Chess Review*, 1950. Reprinted by permission.

annual average rating (if any) are added together—and the result divided by the number of ratings added.

A player's performance rating in a tournament is dependent on two factors: (1) the average rating of the tournament; (2) his score in that tournament. The average rating of a tournament is computed by adding the last performance ratings of all players therein and dividing the sum by the number of contestants.

Performance ratings in round-robin tournaments are calculated as follows: (1) a player who makes a 50% score receives the tournament average as his performance rating; (2) a player who makes a score of more than 50% receives the tournament average plus 10 rating points for each percentage point of his score above average: (3) a player who makes a score of less than 50% receives the tournament average minus 10 rating points for each percentage point of his score below average.

Performance ratings in Swiss-system tournaments are calculated in the same way as in the round-robin tournaments, with one addition: a weighting feature to compensate for the apparent strength of each player's opponents. The average score made by a player's opponents is calculated. Then 10 rating points for each percentage point of this total above or below the tournament average are added or subtracted from the round-robin calculation, in order to determine the performance rating of a player.

The performance rating of a tournament winner is not recorded if it would be impossible for him, even by scoring 100%, to earn a rating at least as high as his last performance rating. If a player's last performance rating is more than 500 points below the average rating of a tournament, a performance rating is not issued to him if he makes a zero score.

The classifications are:

Grandmaster	2700 points and up
Senior master	2500 to 2699 points
Master	2300 to 2499 points
Expert	2100 to 2299 points

Class A	1900 to 2099 points
Class B	1700 to 1899 points
Class C	1500 to 1699 points
Class D	below 1500 points

Chess Etiquette[*]

By Donald MacMurray

Unlike the formal rules of chess, good chess manners do not *have* to be observed. However, this good-humored and sardonic essay, based on actual observation of the foibles of chessplayers, should contribute to higher standards of sportsmanship and fun in chess.

As everyone knows, the worst thing that can happen to a chessplayer is to lose a game. Because this is so, it is evident that what the chess public needs is a method of winning easily without first mastering the difficulty and unnecessary technique of making good moves.

To begin with, you must realize clearly that your principal object is to disturb your opponent as much as possible in order to distract his attention from the game. Of the numerous ways of accomplishing this, the easiest and most common is talking.

Talking to annoy may be done in several ways. You may, for example, talk *to your opponent,* either pointing out bad moves to him, or making any other misleading remark about the position. If your opponent so much as comes near to touching a piece it is always disconcerting to say sternly, "Touch—move." If this involves you in an argument with him, so much the better for your chances of upsetting his train of thought.

An example from actual experience will serve to demonstrate the practicability of this piece of advice. Several years ago, in the interscholastic championship tournament in New York, there arose an endgame position where White, who was on the defensive, had only one way of saving the game, to wit, by pushing a certain Pawn. He permitted his hand to hover over the Pawn, without touching it, whereupon Black cried gleefully, "You touched it!" White denied the charge vigorously, and, when the referee finally decided the fight in his favor, triumphantly proceeded to move another piece, thus losing the game.

You may also talk to the kibitzers, preferably discussing the previous game with them so heatedly that you draw your opponent into the argument, and so take his mind completely off whatever he was considering.

If you like, you may talk *to yourself*. Every chess club boasts at least one genius of the talk-to-yourself school. Curiously enough, the favorite method of these experts is the recitation of nonsense rhymes. The eminent champion of the West has great success in declaiming passages from Lewis Carroll's *Hunting of the Snark;* while one of the most prominent American professionals has confided to me that about half of his yearly income is derived from the recitation, at critical points in his games, of *Mary Had a Little Lamb.*

Another ready means of annoying which you have at your disposal is music. There are several different ways of employing music for this purpose. If you are a timid player, you may try humming, which is the most unobtrusive of the lot, and the least likely to call forth rebuke, but which, when raised to high pitch and accompanied by the gestures of a conductor, will throw your opponent entirely off his game.

As your courage waxes, you will find a shrill, piercing whistle more effective than even the most artistic humming. The tune must be one far too difficult to be whistled correctly, so that it will sound at best like an undecided peanut-roaster.

Finally, being carried away by the beauty of your noises, you may break into full song, accompanying yourself as before, with appropriate gestures, or else by tapping in time with your feet.

If you do not happen to be musically inclined, you will still find a big field open to you in drumming and tapping, either with hands or feet. This is one of the best ways known to induce your opponent to make a hasty move, and is favored by nearly all of the masters who have no confidence in their singing voices.

Other great resources which you possess are coughing, sneezing, and blowing your nose during the progress of the game. These are to be used freely, especially during the wintertime, both as a general distraction and to instill in your adversary the fear of germs.

Similarly, when your opponent does not move quickly enough to suit you (and if you are a right-minded chessplayer, this should be nearly all the time), you should first heave a sigh, then yawn and look at your watch, and finally groan mournfully.

A large class of nuisances not yet touched upon comprises those which aim at distracting the visual attention of the enemy. Of these, the one most highly sanctioned for your adoption is the system of blowing smoke rings across the board. This is useful, not only because it obscures the position, but also because it will surely get into your opponent's eyes or choke him, and thus put him completely at your mercy.

Another annoyance of this type is adjusting pieces which you would like your opponent to take, or else pieces which are on the other side of the board from where your threat is.

If you habitually rest your head on your hand, be certain to keep your elbow constantly on the edge of the board, shifting its position from time to time so as to be always concealing under it at least two or three important squares.

As the evening wears on, you may resort to stretching, in doing which you should take care to fling at least one arm all the way across the board.

Whenever you have what you think is a fairly good position, rock your chair back and forth on its hind legs, assuming meanwhile a complacent attitude, with your thumbs in your vest pockets, as much as to say, "Why do you not resign, you duffer?"

There is only one more kind of disturbance worth mentioning. Although it is infrequent of occurrence, and when it does happen, it is entirely accidental, it is as upsetting as anything else. It is making a strong move.

Bibliography

BOOKS FOR BEGINNERS

José R. Capablanca: *A Primer of Chess*. New York: Harcourt, Brace & Co., 1935.

Larry Evans and Tom Wiswell: *Championship Chess and Checkers For All*. New York: A. S. Barnes & Co., Inc., 1951.

Reuben Fine: *Chess the Easy Way*. New York: David McKay Co., Inc., 1942.*

Kenneth Harkness and Irving Chernev: *Invitation to Chess*. New York: Simon & Schuster, Inc., 1945.

I. A. Horowitz: *Chess for Beginners*. Irvington, N. Y.: Capitol Pub. Co., Inc., 1950.

I. A. Horowitz and Fred Reinfeld: *First Book of Chess*. New York: Sterling Pub. Co., Inc., 1952.

Edward Lasker: *Modern Chess Strategy*. New York: David McKay Co., Inc., 1950.

Edward Lasker: *The Adventure of Chess*. New York: Doubleday & Co., Inc., 1950.

Edward Lasker (Editor): *Mitchell's Guide to the Game of Chess*. New York: David McKay Co., Inc., 1935.

Emanuel Lasker: *How to Play Chess*. New York: Crown Publishers, Inc., 1950.

Fred Reinfeld: *The Complete Chessplayer*. New York: Prentice-Hall, Inc., 1953.

Sammy Reshevsky and Fred Reinfeld: *Learn Chess Fast*. New York: David McKay Co., Inc., 1947.

BOOKS OF MORE ADVANCED INSTRUCTION

José R. Capablanca: *Chess Fundamentals*. New York: Harcourt, Brace & Co., 1938.

* The David McKay Co. was formerly in Philadelphia.

241

R. N. Coles: *Dynamic Chess*. New York: Pitman Pub. Corp., 1956.

I. A. Horowitz and Fred Reinfeld: *How to Improve Your Chess*. New York: E. P. Dutton & Co., Inc., 1952.

Edward Lasker: *Chess for Fun and Chess for Blood*. New York: David McKay Co., Inc., 1942.

Emanuel Lasker: *Common Sense in Chess*. New York: David McKay Co., Inc., 1946.

Aron Nimzovich: *My System*. New York: David McKay Co., Inc., 1947.

Fred Reinfeld: *How to Play Chess Like a Champion*. New York: Doubleday & Co., Inc., 1956.

Fred Reinfeld: *Why You Lose at Chess*. New York: Simon & Schuster, Inc., 1956.

Fred Reinfeld: *Chess for Amateurs*. New York: Pitman Pub. Corp., 1943.

Fred Reinfeld: *Chess Mastery by Question and Answer*. New York: Pitman Pub. Corp., 1939.

Fred Reinfeld: *How to be a Winner at Chess*. New York: Garden City Books, 1954.

Fred Reinfeld: *How to Play Better Chess*. New York: Pitman Pub. Corp., 1948.

Fred Reinfeld: *Second Book of Chess: The Nine Bad Moves and How to Avoid Them*. New York: Sterling Pub. Co., Inc., 1953.

BOOKS ON THE OPENINGS

Irving Chernev: *Winning Chess Traps*. New York: David McKay Co., Inc., 1946.

Reuben Fine: *The Ideas Behind the Chess Openings*. New York: David McKay Co., Inc., 1949.

Reuben Fine (Editor): *Practical Chess Openings*. New York: David McKay Co., Inc., 1948.

I. A. Horowitz: *How to Win in the Chess Openings*. New York: David McKay Co., Inc., 1951.

I. A. Horowitz: *Modern Ideas in the Chess Openings*. New York: David McKay Co., Inc., 1953.

I. A. Horowitz and Fred Reinfeld: *How to Think Ahead in Chess*. New York: Simon & Schuster, Inc., 1951.

Walter Korn (editor): *Modern Chess Openings*. New York: Pitman Pub. Corp., 1952.

E. A. Znosko-Borovsky: *How to Play the Chess Openings*. New York: Pitman Pub. Corp., 1953.

L. Elliott Fletcher: *Gambits Accepted*. New York: D. Van Nostrand Co., Inc., 1955.

BOOKS ON THE MIDDLE GAME

Irving Chernev and Fred Reinfeld: *Winning Chess*. New York: Simon & Schuster, Inc., 1948.

E. Cordingley: *The Next Move Is. . . .* New York: David McKay Co., Inc., 1944.

Dr. Max Euwe: *Strategy and Tactics in Chess*. New York: David McKay Co., Inc., 1948.

Dr. Max Euwe: *Judgment and Planning in Chess*. New York: British Book Centre, Inc., 1952.

Reuben Fine: *The Middle Game in Chess*. New York: David McKay Co., Inc., 1949.

I. A. Horowitz: *How to Win in the Middle Game of Chess*. New York: David McKay Co., Inc., 1955.

I. A. Horowitz and Fred Reinfeld: *Chess Traps, Pitfalls, and Swindles*. New York: Simon & Schuster, Inc., 1954.

Walter Korn: *The Brilliant Touch*. New York: Pitman Publishing Corp., 1950.

Fred Reinfeld: *Challenge to Chessplayers*. New York: David McKay Co., Inc., 1947.

Fred Reinfeld: *Fourth Book of Chess: How to Play the Black Pieces*. New York: Sterling Pub. Co., Inc., 1956.

Fred Reinfeld: *Sixth Book of Chess: How to Fight Back*. New York: Sterling Pub. Co., Inc., 1955.

Fred Reinfeld: *The Elements of Combination Play in Chess*. Irvington, N. Y.: Capitol Pub. Co., Inc., 1950.

Fred Reinfeld: *Third Book of Chess: How to Play the White Pieces*. New York: Sterling Pub. Co., Inc., 1954.

Fred Reinfeld: *1001 Brilliant Chess Sacrifices and Combinations*. New York: Sterling Pub. Co., Inc., 1955.

Fred Reinfeld: *1001 Ways to Checkmate*. New York: Sterling Pub. Co., Inc., 1955.

Georges Renaud and Victor Kahn: *The Art of the Checkmate*. New York: Simon & Schuster, Inc., 1953.

Rudolf Spielmann: *The Art of Sacrifice in Chess*. New York: David McKay Co., Inc., 1951.

E. A. Znosko-Borovsky: *The Middle Game in Chess*. New York: David McKay Co., Inc., 1939

BOOKS ON THE ENDGAME

Irving Chernev: *Chessboard Magic*. New York: David McKay Co., Inc., 1943.

Reuben Fine: *Basic Chess Endings*. New York: David McKay Co., Inc., 1941.

Jacques Mieses: *Manual of the Endgame*. New York: David McKay Co., Inc., 1953.

Fred Reinfeld: *Fifth Book of Chess: How to Win When You're Ahead*. New York: Sterling Pub. Co., Inc., 1955.

INDIVIDUAL GAME COLLECTIONS

C. H. O'D. Alexander: *Alekhine's Best Games of Chess, 1938–1945*. New York: Harcourt, Brace & Co., 1950.

Alexander Alekhine: *My Best Games of Chess, 1908–1923*. New York: Harcourt, Brace & Co., 1939.

Alexander Alekhine: *My Best Games of Chess, 1924–1937*. New York: Harcourt, Brace & Co., 1948.

H. Golombek: *Reti's Best Games of Chess*. New York: D. Van Nostrand Co., Inc., 1956.

George Koltanowski: *Adventures of a Chess Master*. New York: David McKay Co., Inc., 1955.

Frank J. Marshall: *My Fifty Years of Chess*. New York: David McKay Co., Inc., 1942.

Fred Reinfeld: *Tarrasch's Best Games of Chess*. New York: David McKay Co., Inc., 1947.

Fred Reinfeld: *The Immortal Games of Capablanca*. New York: Pitman Pub. Corp., 1942.

Fred Reinfeld: *The Unknown Alekhine*. New York: Pitman Pub. Corp., 1949.

Sammy Reshevsky: *Reshevsky on Chess*. New York: David McKay Co., Inc., 1948.

GENERAL GAME COLLECTIONS

Irving Chernev: *The Russians Play Chess*. New York: David McKay Co., Inc., 1947.

Irving Chernev: *The Thousand Best Short Games of Chess*. New York: Simon & Schuster, Inc., 1955.

R. N. Coles: *Epic Battles of the Chessboard*. New York: David McKay Co., Inc., 1952.

Dr. Max Euwe: *Meet the Masters*. New York: Pitman Pub. Corp., 1946.

Reuben Fine: *Chess Marches On!* New York: David McKay Co., Inc., 1945.

Reuben Fine: *The World's a Chessboard.* New York: David McKay Co., Inc., 1948.

Nicolai Grekov: *Soviet Chess.* New York: David McKay Co., Inc., 1949.

I. A. Horowitz and Hans Kmoch: *World Chessmasters in Battle Royal.* New York: David McKay Co., Inc., 1949.

Hans Kmoch: *New York International Tournament, 1948–1949.* New York: Albert S. Pinkus, 1950.

Edward Lasker: *Chess Secrets.* New York: David McKay Co., Inc., 1951.

Fred Reinfeld: *British Chess Masters.* New York: David McKay Co., Inc., 1947.

Fred Reinfeld and Irving Chernev: *Chess Strategy and Tactics.* New York: David McKay Co., Inc., 1946.

Gideon Stahlberg: *Chess and Chess Masters.* New York: Pitman Pub. Corp., 1956.

Dr. S. Tartakover and J. du Mont: *500 Master Games of Chess.* New York: David McKay Co., Inc., 1954.

Francis J. Wellmuth: *The Golden Treasury of Chess.* New York: David McKay Co., Inc., 1943.

BOOKS FOR ENTERTAINMENT

Assiac: *The Pleasures of Chess.* New York: Simon & Schuster, Inc., 1952.

Irving Chernev: *Curious Chess Facts.* New York: Black Knight Press, 1937.

Irving Chernev: *The Bright Side of Chess.* New York: David McKay Co., Inc., 1948.

Irving Chernev and Fred Reinfeld: *The Fireside Book of Chess.* New York: Simon & Schuster, Inc., 1949.

R. N. Coles: *The Chessplayer's Week-end Book.* New York: Pitman Pub. Corp., 1950.

Alex Hammond: *The Book of Chessmen.* New York: William Morrow & Co., Inc., 1950.

Fred Reinfeld: *The Human Side of Chess.* New York: Pellegrini & Cudahy, Inc., 1952. (Reissued as *The Great Chess Masters and Their Games.* New York: Sterling Pub. Co., Inc., 1955.)

Fred Reinfeld (Editor): *The Treasury of Chess Lore.* New York: David McKay Co., Inc., 1951.

Index